The Lake District
214 Peak Challenge Log
'Bagging the Wainw~

Peak or mountain 'Bagging' is an ever increas~ ... ple of all ages and abilities. Not only a great wa~ ... activity wether you choose to do it alone or with ~ ... ~thing quite like the feeling when you have reached ... ~ out over the spectacular views!

There is arguably no better place to 'bag' pe~ ... _ake District - with the popular 'Wainwrights' being the most popular c~ ... . This log book is for you to document your own bagging journey, all 214 of ~ ... ~ainwrights are listed in this book for you to plan, document and subsequently look back on your adventures.

Scanning a QR code

Using a smartphone, search for a 'QR reader' - there a numerous free ones available to download to your phone. Once downloaded, open the app and point the camera at the code on each mountain and this will open up the wiki page for that particular mountain with loads of information to plan your trip!

A note from the author....

Growing up in Cumbria has meant I have been in the privileged position of being only a 30 minute drive away from the lakes, so have enjoyed a lot of the beauty it has to offer. It certainly is a place that everyone in the UK should experience at least once! Having been 'bagging' my peaks for the last 5 years, I wished that I had documented them as I go - so I decided to create this log book for like minded baggers. Retailing mainly on Amazon, I must say the response to the book has been phenomenal, so a huge thank you for your support.

I am constantly looking to evolve the book and this last update is quite a substantial one. Now the mountains have been listed in region order rather than height ascending. This means that you can complete the regions one by one - and the new maps at the beginning of each section allow you to colour in the peaks as you complete them. I have expanded the contents section so you can easily find your mountain by name, region or height ascending order.

At the back of this edition are some vouchers offered by local businesses. These offers have been exclusively given to this book, so simply cut out the vouchers and redeem them at the venue.

I hope you enjoy this latest revision of the book, and if you have any further suggestions of improvements please feel free to email me at: info@herbertpublishing.com and I will see what I can do.

Lastly, leaving a review on Amazon for this book really helps independent publishers, so would really appreciate a review! - now off you go and plan your next hike!!!!

Thanks so much
Lee Herbert
Herbert Publishing_

Fell Finder - In Alphabetical Order

Fell Finder - In Alphabetical Order

Fell Finder - In Region Order

Fell Finder - Height Ascending Order

Height (ft)	Mountain	Page	Height (ft)	Mountain	Page	Height (ft)	Mountain	Page
951 ft	Castle Crag	Page 104	1,864 ft	Outerside	Page 117	2,415 ft	Harrison Stickle	Page 26
1,040 ft	Holme Fell	Page 160	1,873 ft	Sergeant's Crag	Page 18	2,415 ft	Sergeant Man	Page 27
1,060 ft	Black Fell	Page 161	1,880 ft	Blake Fell	Page 202	2,417 ft	Seat Sandal	Page 48
1,099 ft	Loughrigg Fell	Page 2	1,886 ft	Maiden Moor	Page 118	2,418 ft	Robinson	Page 125
1,165 ft	Rannerdale Knotts	Page 105	1,890 ft	The Nab	Page 77	2,425 ft	The Knott (High Street)	Page 92
1,171 ft	High Rigg (Naddle Fell)	Page 3	1,906 ft	Hartsop above How	Page 39	2,441 ft	High Crag	Page 214
1,178 ft	Sale Fell	Page 106	1,906 ft	Ard Crags	Page 116	2,448 ft	Carl Side	Page 154
1,194 ft	Troutbeck Tongue	Page 66	1,909 ft	Middle Fell	Page 204	2,470 ft	Dale Head	Page 126
1,207 ft	Latrigg	Page 134	1,923 ft	Brae Fell	Page 141	2,477 ft	Red Pike (Buttermere)	Page 215
1,224 ft	Ling Fell	Page 107	1,926 ft	Shipman Knotts	Page 78	2,480 ft	Hart Side	Page 49
1,243 ft	Walla Crag	Page 4	1,936 ft	Bleaberry Fell	Page 19	2,484 ft	Ill Bell	Page 93
1,273 ft	Hallin Fell	Page 67	1,959 ft	Haystacks	Page 203	2,493 ft	Mardale Ill Bell	Page 94
1,294 ft	Silver How	Page 5	1,972 ft	Seathwaite Fell	Page 167	2,500 ft	High Raise (Langdale)	Page 28
1,329 ft	Helm Crag	Page 6	1,995 ft	High Seat	Page 20	2,500 ft	Slight Side	Page 173
1,365 ft	Grange Fell (Brund Fell)	Page 7	1,998 ft	Illgill Head	Page 168	2,503 ft	Stony Cove Pike (Caudale Moor)	Page 95
1,365 ft	Fellbarrow (Mosser Fell)	Page 193	2,008 ft	Heron Pike (Rydal)	Page 40	2,503 ft	Wetherlam	Page 174
1,378 ft	Gibson Knott	Page 8	2,021 ft	Great Borne	Page 205	2,513 ft	Great Rigg	Page 50
1,388 ft	Buckbarrow	Page 194	2,028 ft	Hartsop Dodd	Page 79	2,526 ft	Hopegill Head	Page 127
1,388 ft	Low Fell	Page 192	2,041 ft	Birks	Page 41	2,533 ft	Wandope	Page 129
1,417 ft	Steel Knotts	Page 68	2,057 ft	Yewbarrow	Page 206	2,536 ft	Sail	Page 128
1,421 ft	Arnison Crag	Page 30	2,077 ft	Mungrisdale Common	Page 142	2,536 ft	Grey Friar	Page 175
1,450 ft	Glenridding Dodd	Page 31	2,077 ft	Starling Dodd	Page 207	2,544 ft	Red Screes	Page 51
1,467 ft	Binsey	Page 135	2,090 ft	Little Hart Crag (West Top)	Page 42	2,552 ft	Dow Crag	Page 176
1,473 ft	Great Crag (Stonethwaite)	Page 9	2,090 ft	Causey Pike	Page 119	2,556 ft	Harter Fell (Mardale)	Page 96
1,476 ft	Nab Scar	Page 32	2,093 ft	Grey Crag (Sleddale)	Page 80	2,559 ft	Kidsty Pike	Page 97
1,480 ft	Catbells	Page 109	2,119 ft	Base Brown	Page 208	2,569 ft	Glaramara	Page 177
1,483 ft	Graystones	Page 108	2,129 ft	Fleetwith Pike	Page 209	2,572 ft	Thornthwaite Crag	Page 98
1,493 ft	Barrow	Page 110	2,136 ft	Great Sca Fell	Page 143	2,575 ft	Allen Crags	Page 178
1,512 ft	Raven Crag	Page 10	2,136 ft	Rosset Pike	Page 169	2,575 ft	Great Carrs	Page 179
1,539 ft	Barf	Page 111	2,143 ft	High Spy	Page 120	2,589 ft	Watson's Dodd	Page 52
1,542 ft	Lingmoor Fell	Page 162	2,146 ft	Middle Dodd	Page 43	2,595 ft	Grisedale Pike	Page 130
1,558 ft	Armboth Fell	Page 11	2,146 ft	Harter Fell (Eskdale)	Page 170	2,598 ft	Dove Crag	Page 53
1,558 ft	Burnbank Fell	Page 195	2,149 ft	Selside Pike	Page 81	2,598 ft	Rampsgill Head	Page 99
1,579 ft	Gowbarrow Fell	Page 33	2,152 ft	High Pike (Scandale)	Page 44	2,612 ft	Brim Fell	Page 180
1,585 ft	Sour Howes	Page 69	2,156 ft	Place Fell	Page 82	2,615 ft	Haycock	Page 217
1,585 ft	Longlands Fell	Page 136	2,159 ft	High Pike (Caldbeck)	Page 144	2,628 ft	Green Gable	Page 216
1,597 ft	Baystones (Wansfell)	Page 70	2,165 ft	Whiteless Pike	Page 121	2,631 ft	High Raise (High Street)	Page 100
1,601 ft	Grike	Page 196	2,175 ft	Carrock Fell	Page 145	2,633 ft	Old Man of Coniston	Page 182
1,603 ft	Green Crag	Page 163	2,178 ft	Tarn Crag (Sleddale)	Page 83	2,633 ft	Swirl How	Page 181
1,647 ft	Dodd (Skiddaw)	Page 137	2,201 ft	Wether Hill	Page 85	2,631 ft	Kirk Fell	Page 218
1,654 ft	Stone Arthur	Page 34	2,205 ft	Loadpot Hill	Page 84	2,644 ft	High Stile	Page 219
1,657 ft	Little Mell Fell	Page 35	2,205 ft	Scar Crags	Page 122	2,648 ft	Lingmell	Page 183
1,667 ft	Low Pike	Page 36	2,208 ft	Bakestall	Page 146	2,687 ft	Steeple	Page 220
1,670 ft	Beda Fell (Beda Head)	Page 71	2,215 ft	Sheffield Pike	Page 45	2,697 ft	Hart Crag	Page 54
1,670 ft	Hen Comb	Page 197	2,231 ft	Loft Crag	Page 21	2,710 ft	Red Pike (Wasdale)	Page 221
1,677 ft	Broom Fell	Page 112	2,241 ft	Bannerdale Crags	Page 147	2,717 ft	High Street	Page 101
1,680 ft	Mellbreak	Page 198	2,264 ft	Great Calva	Page 149	2,753 ft	Crag Hill (Eel Crag)	Page 131
1,690 ft	High Tove	Page 13	2,264 ft	Ullock Pike	Page 148	2,759 ft	St Sunday Crag	Page 55
1,693 ft	Sallows	Page 72	2,270 ft	Seatallan	Page 210	2,759 ft	Scoat Fell	Page 222
1,696 ft	Whinlatter (Brown How)	Page 113	2,283 ft	Rest Dodd	Page 86	2,766 ft	Stybarrow Dodd	Page 56
1,703 ft	High Hartsop Dodd	Page 37	2,287 ft	Caw Fell	Page 212	2,795 ft	Grasmoor	Page 132
1,713 ft	Souther Fell	Page 138	2,287 ft	Grey Knotts	Page 211	2,812 ft	Great Dodd	Page 57
1,714 ft	Crag Fell	Page 199	2,293 ft	Gray Crag	Page 87	2,815 ft	Dollywaggon Pike	Page 58
1,719 ft	Bonscale Pike	Page 73	2,297 ft	Pavey Ark	Page 22	2,818 ft	Crinkle Crags (Long Top)	Page 184
1,722 ft	Eagle Crag	Page 12	2,300 ft	Cold Pike	Page 171	2,831 ft	White Side	Page 59
1,726 ft	Great Cockup	Page 139	2,303 ft	Bowscale Fell	Page 150	2,838 ft	Skiddaw Little Man	Page 155
1,726 ft	Gavel Fell	Page 200	2,313 ft	Pike of Blisco	Page 172	2,848 ft	Blencathra (Hallsfell Top)	Page 156
1,749 ft	Arthur's Pike	Page 74	2,316 ft	Yoke	Page 88	2,864 ft	Fairfield	Page 60
1,762 ft	Calf Crag	Page 14	2,320 ft	Whiteside (West Top)	Page 123	2,897 ft	Raise	Page 61
1,762 ft	Great Mell Fell	Page 38	2,326 ft	Pike of Stickle	Page 23	2,904 ft	Esk Pike	Page 185
1,762 ft	Whin Rigg	Page 164	2,329 ft	Knott	Page 151	2,920 ft	Catstye cam	Page 62
1,775 ft	Blea Rigg	Page 15	2,339 ft	Branstree	Page 89	2,923 ft	Nethermost Pike	Page 63
1,775 ft	Lank Rigg	Page 201	2,346 ft	Lonscale Fell	Page 152	2,927 ft	Pillar	Page 223
1,801 ft	Tarn Crag (Easedale)	Page 16	2,346 ft	Brandreth	Page 213	2,949 ft	Great Gable	Page 224
1,801 ft	Hard Knott	Page 165	2,356 ft	Birkhouse Moor	Page 46	2,962 ft	Bowfell	Page 186
1,804 ft	Meal Fell	Page 140	2,362 ft	Froswick	Page 90	2,984 ft	Great End	Page 187
1,808 ft	Rosthwaite Fell	Page 166	2,372 ft	Thunacar Knott	Page 24	3,054 ft	Skiddaw	Page 157
1,811 ft	Lord's Seat	Page 115	2,382 ft	Ullscarf	Page 25	3,117 ft	Helvellyn	Page 64
1,814 ft	Steel Fell (Dead Pike)	Page 17	2,382 ft	Clough Head	Page 47	3,162 ft	Scafell	Page 188
1,824 ft	Knott Rigg	Page 114	2,385 ft	Hindscarth	Page 124	3,209 ft	Scafell Pike	Page 189
1,841 ft	Brock Crags	Page 75	2,395 ft	Kentmere Pike	Page 91			
1,860 ft	Angletarn Pikes (North Top)	Page 76	2,408 ft	Long Side	Page 153			

My Equipment Checklist

- _____ ☐
- _____ ☐
- _____ ☐
- _____ ☐
- _____ ☐
- _____ ☐
- _____ ☐
- _____ ☐
- _____ ☐
- _____ ☐
- _____ ☐
- _____ ☐
- _____ ☐
- _____ ☐
- _____ ☐
- _____ ☐
- _____ ☐
- _____ ☐
- _____ ☐
- _____ ☐

- _____ ☐
- _____ ☐
- _____ ☐
- _____ ☐
- _____ ☐
- _____ ☐
- _____ ☐
- _____ ☐
- _____ ☐
- _____ ☐
- _____ ☐
- _____ ☐
- _____ ☐
- _____ ☐
- _____ ☐
- _____ ☐
- _____ ☐
- _____ ☐
- _____ ☐

THE LAKE DISTRICT NATIONAL PARK
(AND SOME OF ITS MOST POPULAR MOUNTAINS)

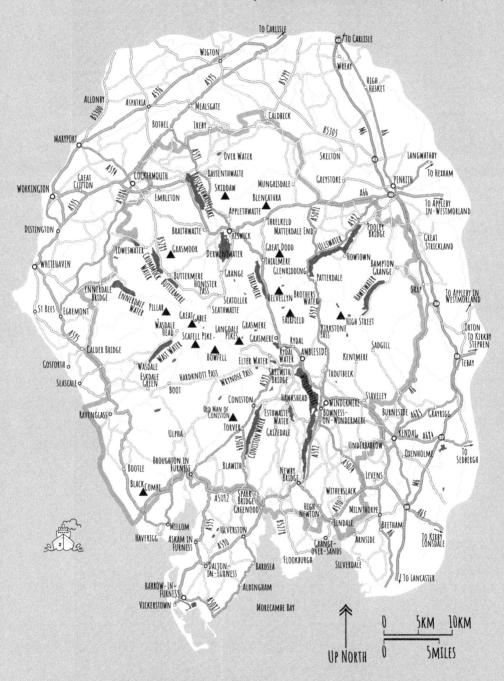

To Carlisle · To Carlisle · Wigton · Wreay · High Hesket · Allonby · Aspatria · Mealsgate · Caldbeck · B5299 · B5305 · Langwathby · Maryport · Bothel · Ireby · Over Water · Skelton · Greystoke · A595 · A591 · To Hexham · Workington · Great Clifton · Cockermouth · Bassenthwaite · Embleton · Bassenthwaite Lake · Skiddaw · Mungrisdale · Blencathra · Applethwaite · Penrith · A66 · To Appleby in-Westmorland · Great Strickland · Distington · Braithwaite · Threlkeld · Matterdale End · A5091 · Pooley Bridge · Whitehaven · Loweswater · Grasmoor · Keswick · Derwentwater · Great Dodd · Ullswater · Howtown · Bampton Grange · Buttermere · Thirlmere · Glenridding · Patterdale · Haweswater · St Bees · Ennerdale Bridge · Crummock Water · Honister Pass · Grange · Helvellyn · Brothers Water · Shap · To Appleby in Westmorland · Egremont · Ennerdale Water · Pillar · Seatoller · Seathwaite · Fairfield · High Street · Kirkstone Pass · Orton To Kirkby Stephen · Calder Bridge · Wasdale Head · Great Gable · Langdale Pikes · Grasmere · Rydal · Sadgill · Tebay · Gosforth · Scafell Pike · Bowfell · Grasmere · Rydal Water · Ambleside · Kentmere · Seascale · Wast Water · Wasdale · Elter Water · Skelwith Bridge · Troutbeck · Staveley · Ravenglass · Eskdale Green · Hardknott Pass · Wrynose Pass · Hawkshead · Windermere · Burneside · Grayrigg · Boot · Coniston · Esthwaite Water · Bowness-on-Windermere · Kendal · Old Man of Coniston · Torver · Grizedale · Underbarrow · Oxenholme · Ulpha · Coniston Water · To Sedbergh · Broughton in Furness · Blawith · Newby Bridge · Levens · Bootle · Witherslack · Milnthorpe · Beetham · Black Combe · Park Bridge Greenodd · High Newton · Lindale · Arnside · To Kirkby Lonsdale · Millom · Ulverston · Grange-over-Sands · Silverdale · Haverigg · Askam in Furness · A590 · Bardsea · Flookburgh · To Lancaster · Dalton-in-Furness · Aldingham · Barrow-in-Furness · Vickerstown · Morecambe Bay

Up North

0   5KM   10KM
0   5MILES

~~~ NATIONAL PARK BOUNDARY

Also available on Amazon...

A Wainwright bagging logbook for kids and juniors! A great logbook for enthusiastic youngsters to journal all their adventures in the lakes, with every Wainwright listed in the book to complete. A great way for the whole family to enjoy & record their days out in the fabulous Lake District for years to come!

To buy this book, search for
"BO8X6C6X2M"
on Amazon.co.uk

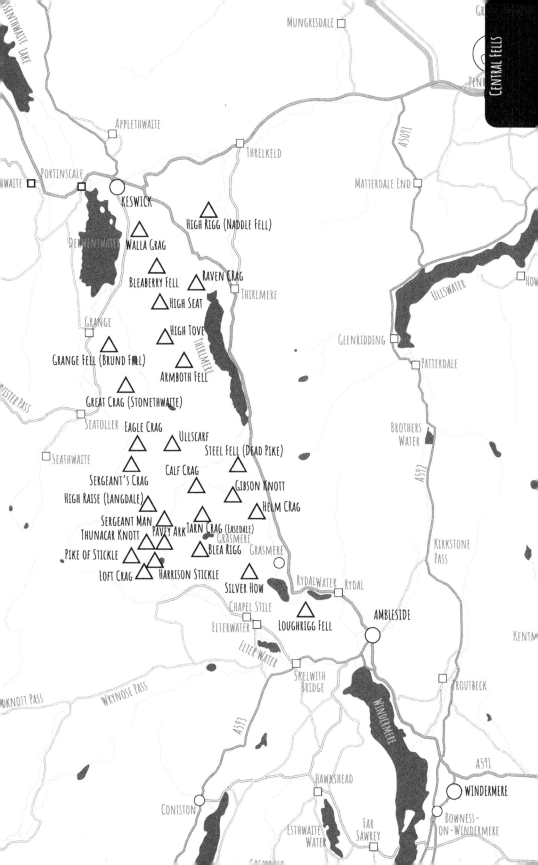

MUNGRISDALE

APPLETHWAITE

THRELKELD

MATTERDALE END

KESWICK

PORTINSCALE

PENR...

GLENRIDDING

PATTERDALE

ULLSWATER

HIGH RIGG (NADDLE FELL)

WALLA CRAG

DERWENTWATER

BLEABERRY FELL

RAVEN CRAG

THIRLMERE

HIGH SEAT

HIGH TOVE

GRANGE

THIRLMERE

GRANGE FELL (BRUND FELL)

ARMBOTH FELL

BROTHERS WATER

GREAT CRAG (STONETHWAITE)

STER PASS

SEATOLLER

EAGLE CRAG

SEATHWAITE

ULLSCARF

STEEL FELL (DEAD PIKE)

CALF CRAG

SERGEANT'S CRAG

GIBSON KNOTT

HIGH RAISE (LANGDALE)

HELM CRAG

A592

KIRKSTONE PASS

SERGEANT MAN

TARN CRAG (EASEDALE)

THUNACAR KNOTT

PAVEY ARK

GRASMERE

PIKE OF STICKLE

BLEA RIGG

GRASMERE

LOFT CRAG

HARRISON STICKLE

SILVER HOW

RYDALWATER

RYDAL

CHAPEL STILE

AMBLESIDE

ELTERWATER

LOUGHRIGG FELL

KENTM

ELTER WATER

SKELWITH BRIDGE

TROUTBECK

DKNOTT PASS

WRYNOSE PASS

A593

WINDERMERE

A591

WINDERMERE

CONISTON

HAWKSHEAD

BOWNESS-ON-WINDERMERE

ESTHWAITE WATER

FAR SAWREY

Loughrigg Fell
Region: Central Fells
Height: 335m / 1,099ft
OS Grid Ref: NY346051

Date: ....

Ascent start time: .... Peak time: ....

Descent start time: .... Finish time: ....

Ascent duration: .... Descent duration: ....

Total time: [   ]

Total distance covered:..

Companions:...
....

Local Pub: .... ☆ ☆ ☆ ☆ ☆

Weather conditions:...
....

Difficulty: (poor) ○ ○ ○ ○ ○ ○ ○ ○ ○ (great)

Views: (poor) ○ ○ ○ ○ ○ ○ ○ ○ ○ (great)

Enjoyment: (poor) ○ ○ ○ ○ ○ ○ ○ ○ ○ (great)

Notes/pics:

High Rigg (Naddle Fell)

Region: Central Fells
Height: 357m / 1,171ft
OS Grid Ref: NY308219

Date: ....

Ascent start time: .... Peak time: ....

Descent start time: .... Finish time: ....

Ascent duration: .... Descent duration: ....

Total time: [   ]

Total distance covered:..

Companions:..

....

Local Pub: .... ☆ ☆ ☆ ☆ ☆

Weather conditions:..

....

Difficulty: (poor) ○ ○ ○ ○ ○ ○ ○ ○ ○ (great)

Views: (poor) ○ ○ ○ ○ ○ ○ ○ ○ ○ (great)

Enjoyment: (poor) ○ ○ ○ ○ ○ ○ ○ ○ ○ (great)

Notes/pics:

Walla Crag

Region: Central Fells
Height: 379m / 1,243ft
OS Grid Ref: NY276212

Date: ....

Ascent start time: .... Peak time: ....

Descent start time: .... Finish time: ....

Ascent duration: .... Descent duration: ....

Total time: [   ]

Total distance covered:...

Companions:...

....

Local Pub: .... ☆ ☆ ☆ ☆ ☆

Weather conditions:...

....

Difficulty: (poor) ○ ○ ○ ○ ○ ○ ○ ○ ○ ○ (great)

Views: (poor) ○ ○ ○ ○ ○ ○ ○ ○ ○ ○ (great)

Enjoyment: (poor) ○ ○ ○ ○ ○ ○ ○ ○ ○ ○ (great)

Notes/pics:

Silver How

Region: Central Fells
Height: 395m / 1,296ft
OS Grid Ref: NY324066

Date: ....

Ascent start time: .... Peak time: ....

Descent start time: .... Finish time: ....

Ascent duration: .... Descent duration: ....

Total time: [   ]

Total distance covered:..

Companions:...

....

Local Pub: .... ☆☆☆☆☆

Weather conditions:...

....

Difficulty: (poor) ○ ○ ○ ○ ○ ○ ○ ○ ○ ○ (great)

Views: (poor) ○ ○ ○ ○ ○ ○ ○ ○ ○ ○ (great)

Enjoyment: (poor) ○ ○ ○ ○ ○ ○ ○ ○ ○ ○ (great)

Notes/pics:

Helm Crag

Region: Central Fells
Height: 405m / 1,329ft
OS Grid Ref: NY326093

Date: ....

Ascent start time: .... Peak time: ....

Descent start time: .... Finish time: ....

Ascent duration: .... Descent duration: ....

Total time: [   ]

Total distance covered:..

Companions:..

....

Local Pub: .... ☆ ☆ ☆ ☆ ☆

Weather conditions:...

....

Difficulty: (poor) ○ ○ ○ ○ ○ ○ ○ ○ ○ (great)

Views: (poor) ○ ○ ○ ○ ○ ○ ○ ○ ○ (great)

Enjoyment: (poor) ○ ○ ○ ○ ○ ○ ○ ○ ○ (great)

Notes/pics:

Grange Fell (Brund Fell)

Region: Central Fells
Height: 416m / 1,365ft
OS Grid Ref: NY264162

Date: ....

Ascent start time: .... Peak time: ....

Descent start time: .... Finish time: ....

Ascent duration: .... Descent duration: ....

Total time: [   ]

Total distance covered:...

Companions:..

....

Local Pub: .... ☆ ☆ ☆ ☆ ☆

Weather conditions:...

....

Difficulty: (poor) ○ ○ ○ ○ ○ ○ ○ ○ ○ (great)

Views: (poor) ○ ○ ○ ○ ○ ○ ○ ○ ○ (great)

Enjoyment: (poor) ○ ○ ○ ○ ○ ○ ○ ○ ○ (great)

Notes/pics:

Gibson Knott

Region: Central Fells
Height: 420m / 1,378ft
OS Grid Ref: NY316100

Date: ....

Ascent start time: .... Peak time: ....

Descent start time: .... Finish time: ....

Ascent duration: .... Descent duration: ....

Total time: [   ]

Total distance covered:...

Companions:...

....

Local Pub: .... ☆ ☆ ☆ ☆ ☆

Weather conditions:..

....

Difficulty: (poor) ○ ○ ○ ○ ○ ○ ○ ○ ○ ○ (great)

Views: (poor) ○ ○ ○ ○ ○ ○ ○ ○ ○ ○ (great)

Enjoyment: (poor) ○ ○ ○ ○ ○ ○ ○ ○ ○ ○ (great)

Notes/pics:

Great Crag (Stonethwaite)

Region: Central Fells
Height: 449m / 1,473ft
OS Grid Ref: NY270146

Date: ....

Ascent start time: .... Peak time: ....

Descent start time: .... Finish time: ....

Ascent duration: .... Descent duration: ....

Total time: [   ]

Total distance covered:...

Companions:...

....

Local Pub: .... ☆☆☆☆☆

Weather conditions:...

....

Difficulty: (poor) ○ ○ ○ ○ ○ ○ ○ ○ ○ (great)

Views: (poor) ○ ○ ○ ○ ○ ○ ○ ○ ○ (great)

Enjoyment: (poor) ○ ○ ○ ○ ○ ○ ○ ○ ○ (great)

Notes/pics:

Raven Crag

Region: Central Fells
Height: 461m / 1,512ft
OS Grid Ref: NY303187

Date: ....

Ascent start time: .... Peak time: ....

Descent start time: .... Finish time: ....

Ascent duration: .... Descent duration: ....

Total time: [   ]

Total distance covered:...

Companions:...

....

Local Pub: .... ☆ ☆ ☆ ☆ ☆

Weather conditions:..

....

Difficulty: (poor) ○ ○ ○ ○ ○ ○ ○ ○ ○ (great)

Views: (poor) ○ ○ ○ ○ ○ ○ ○ ○ ○ (great)

Enjoyment: (poor) ○ ○ ○ ○ ○ ○ ○ ○ ○ (great)

Notes/pics:

Armboth Fell

Region: Central Fells
Height: 475m / 1,558ft
OS Grid Ref: NY295157

Date: ....

Ascent start time: .... Peak time: ....

Descent start time: .... Finish time: ....

Ascent duration: .... Descent duration: ....

Total time: [   ]

Total distance covered:...

Companions:...

....

Local Pub: .... ☆☆☆☆☆

Weather conditions:...

....

Difficulty: (poor) ○ ○ ○ ○ ○ ○ ○ ○ ○ (great)

Views: (poor) ○ ○ ○ ○ ○ ○ ○ ○ ○ (great)

Enjoyment: (poor) ○ ○ ○ ○ ○ ○ ○ ○ ○ (great)

Notes/pics:

11

Eagle Crag

Region: Central Fells
Height: 525m / 1,722ft
OS Grid Ref: NY275121

Date: ....

Ascent start time: .... Peak time: ....

Descent start time: .... Finish time: ....

Ascent duration: .... Descent duration: ....

Total time: [   ]

Total distance covered:..

Companions:...

....

Local Pub: .... ☆ ☆ ☆ ☆ ☆

Weather conditions:...

....

Difficulty: (poor) ⭘ ⭘ ⭘ ⭘ ⭘ ⭘ ⭘ ⭘ ⭘ (great)

Views: (poor) ⭘ ⭘ ⭘ ⭘ ⭘ ⭘ ⭘ ⭘ ⭘ (great)

Enjoyment: (poor) ⭘ ⭘ ⭘ ⭘ ⭘ ⭘ ⭘ ⭘ ⭘ (great)

Notes/pics:

High Tove

Region: Central Fells
Height: 515m / 1,690ft
OS Grid Ref: NY289165

Date: ....

Ascent start time: .... Peak time: ....

Descent start time: .... Finish time: ....

Ascent duration: .... Descent duration: ....

Total time: [   ]

Total distance covered:...

Companions:...

....

Local Pub: .... ☆☆☆☆☆

Weather conditions:..

....

Difficulty: (poor) ○ ○ ○ ○ ○ ○ ○ ○ ○ (great)

Views: (poor) ○ ○ ○ ○ ○ ○ ○ ○ ○ (great)

Enjoyment: (poor) ○ ○ ○ ○ ○ ○ ○ ○ ○ (great)

Notes/pics:

Calf Crag

Region: Central Fells
Height: 537m / 1,762ft
OS Grid Ref: NY301104

Date: ....

Ascent start time: .... Peak time: ....

Descent start time: .... Finish time: ....

Ascent duration: .... Descent duration: ....

Total time: [   ]

Total distance covered:...

Companions:..

....

Local Pub: .... ☆☆☆☆☆

Weather conditions:..

....

Difficulty: (poor) ○ ○ ○ ○ ○ ○ ○ ○ ○ (great)

Views: (poor) ○ ○ ○ ○ ○ ○ ○ ○ ○ (great)

Enjoyment: (poor) ○ ○ ○ ○ ○ ○ ○ ○ ○ (great)

Notes/pics:

Blea Rigg

Region: Central Fells
Height: 541m / 1,775ft
OS Grid Ref: NY301078

Date: ....

Ascent start time: .... Peak time: ....

Descent start time: .... Finish time: ....

Ascent duration: .... Descent duration: ....

Total time: [   ]

Total distance covered:..

Companions:...
....

Local Pub: .... ☆☆☆☆☆

Weather conditions:..
....

Difficulty: (poor) ○ ○ ○ ○ ○ ○ ○ ○ ○ ○ (great)

Views: (poor) ○ ○ ○ ○ ○ ○ ○ ○ ○ ○ (great)

Enjoyment: (poor) ○ ○ ○ ○ ○ ○ ○ ○ ○ ○ (great)

Notes/pics:

Tarn Crag (Easedale)

Region: Central Fells
Height: 549m / 1,801ft
OS Grid Ref: NY303093

Date: ....

Ascent start time: .... Peak time: ....

Descent start time: .... Finish time: ....

Ascent duration: .... Descent duration: ....

Total time: [   ]

Total distance covered:..

Companions:..

....

Local Pub: .... ☆ ☆ ☆ ☆ ☆

Weather conditions:...

....

Difficulty: (poor) ○ ○ ○ ○ ○ ○ ○ ○ ○ (great)

Views: (poor) ○ ○ ○ ○ ○ ○ ○ ○ ○ (great)

Enjoyment: (poor) ○ ○ ○ ○ ○ ○ ○ ○ ○ (great)

Notes/pics:

Steel Fell (Dead Pike)

Region: Central Fells
Height: 553m / 1,814ft
OS Grid Ref: NY319111

Date: ....

Ascent start time: .... Peak time: ....

Descent start time: .... Finish time: ....

Ascent duration: .... Descent duration: ....

Total time: [   ]

Total distance covered: ....

Companions: ....

....

Local Pub: .... ☆ ☆ ☆ ☆ ☆

Weather conditions: ....

....

Difficulty: (poor) ○ ○ ○ ○ ○ ○ ○ ○ ○ (great)

Views: (poor) ○ ○ ○ ○ ○ ○ ○ ○ ○ (great)

Enjoyment: (poor) ○ ○ ○ ○ ○ ○ ○ ○ ○ (great)

Notes/pics:

Sergeant's Crag

Region: Central Fells
Height: 571m / 1,873ft
OS Grid Ref: NY273113

Date: ....

Ascent start time: .... Peak time: ....

Descent start time: .... Finish time: ....

Ascent duration: .... Descent duration: ....

Total time: [   ]

Total distance covered:...

Companions:..

....

Local Pub: .... ☆ ☆ ☆ ☆ ☆

Weather conditions:..

....

Difficulty: (poor) ○ ○ ○ ○ ○ ○ ○ ○ ○ (great)

Views: (poor) ○ ○ ○ ○ ○ ○ ○ ○ ○ (great)

Enjoyment: (poor) ○ ○ ○ ○ ○ ○ ○ ○ ○ (great)

Notes/pics:

Bleaberry Fell

Region: Central Fells
Height: 590m / 1,936ft
OS Grid Ref: NY285195

Date: ....

Ascent start time: .... Peak time: ....

Descent start time: .... Finish time: ....

Ascent duration: .... Descent duration: ....

Total time: [ ]

Total distance covered:...

Companions:...

....

Local Pub: .... ☆ ☆ ☆ ☆ ☆

Weather conditions:..

....

Difficulty: (poor) ○ ○ ○ ○ ○ ○ ○ ○ ○ ○ (great)

Views: (poor) ○ ○ ○ ○ ○ ○ ○ ○ ○ ○ (great)

Enjoyment: (poor) ○ ○ ○ ○ ○ ○ ○ ○ ○ ○ (great)

Notes/pics:

High Seat

Region: Central Fells
Height: 608m / 1,995ft
OS Grid Ref: NY287180

Date: ....

Ascent start time: .... Peak time: ....

Descent start time: .... Finish time: ....

Ascent duration: .... Descent duration: ....

Total time: [   ]

Total distance covered:...

Companions:...

....

Local Pub: .... ☆☆☆☆☆

Weather conditions:...

....

Difficulty: (poor) ○○○○○○○○○ (great)

Views: (poor) ○○○○○○○○○ (great)

Enjoyment: (poor) ○○○○○○○○○ (great)

Notes/pics:

Loft Crag

Region: Central Fells
Height: 680m / 2,231ft
OS Grid Ref: NY277071

Date: ....

Ascent start time: .... Peak time: ....

Descent start time: .... Finish time: ....

Ascent duration: .... Descent duration: ....

Total time: [   ]

Total distance covered:...

Companions:...
....

Local Pub: .... ☆☆☆☆☆

Weather conditions:...
....

Difficulty: (poor) ○ ○ ○ ○ ○ ○ ○ ○ ○ (great)

Views: (poor) ○ ○ ○ ○ ○ ○ ○ ○ ○ (great)

Enjoyment: (poor) ○ ○ ○ ○ ○ ○ ○ ○ ○ (great)

Notes/pics:

Pavey Ark

Region: Central Fells
Height: 700m / 2,297ft
OS Grid Ref: NY284079

Date: ....

Ascent start time: .... Peak time: ....

Descent start time: .... Finish time: ....

Ascent duration: .... Descent duration: ....

Total time: [   ]

Total distance covered:...

Companions:..

....

Local Pub: .... ☆ ☆ ☆ ☆ ☆

Weather conditions:...

....

Difficulty: (poor) ○ ○ ○ ○ ○ ○ ○ ○ ○ ○ (great)

Views: (poor) ○ ○ ○ ○ ○ ○ ○ ○ ○ ○ (great)

Enjoyment: (poor) ○ ○ ○ ○ ○ ○ ○ ○ ○ ○ (great)

Notes/pics:

Pike of Stickle

Region: Central Fells
Height: 709m / 2,326ft
OS Grid Ref: NY273073

Date: ....

Ascent start time: .... Peak time: ....

Descent start time: .... Finish time: ....

Ascent duration: .... Descent duration: ....

Total time: [   ]

Total distance covered: ....

Companions: ....

....

Local Pub: .... ☆☆☆☆☆

Weather conditions: ....

....

Difficulty: (poor) ○ ○ ○ ○ ○ ○ ○ ○ ○ (great)

Views: (poor) ○ ○ ○ ○ ○ ○ ○ ○ ○ (great)

Enjoyment: (poor) ○ ○ ○ ○ ○ ○ ○ ○ ○ (great)

Notes/pics:

Thunacar Knott

Region: Central Fells
Height: 723m / 2,372ft
OS Grid Ref: NY279079

Date: ....

Ascent start time: .... Peak time: ....

Descent start time: .... Finish time: ....

Ascent duration: .... Descent duration: ....

Total time: [   ]

Total distance covered:..

Companions:..

....

Local Pub: .... ☆☆☆☆☆

Weather conditions:...

....

Difficulty: (poor) ○ ○ ○ ○ ○ ○ ○ ○ ○ (great)

Views: (poor) ○ ○ ○ ○ ○ ○ ○ ○ ○ (great)

Enjoyment: (poor) ○ ○ ○ ○ ○ ○ ○ ○ ○ (great)

Notes/pics:

Ullscarf

Region: Central Fells
Height: 726m / 2,382ft
OS Grid Ref: NY291121

Date: ....

Ascent start time: .... Peak time: ....

Descent start time: .... Finish time: ....

Ascent duration: .... Descent duration: ....

Total time: [   ]

Total distance covered:...

Companions:...

....

Local Pub: .... ☆☆☆☆☆

Weather conditions:...

....

Difficulty: (poor) ○ ○ ○ ○ ○ ○ ○ ○ ○ (great)

Views: (poor) ○ ○ ○ ○ ○ ○ ○ ○ ○ (great)

Enjoyment: (poor) ○ ○ ○ ○ ○ ○ ○ ○ ○ (great)

Notes/pics:

Harrison Stickle

Region: Central Fells
Height: 736m / 2,415ft
OS Grid Ref: NY281074

Date: ....

Ascent start time: .... Peak time: ....

Descent start time: .... Finish time: ....

Ascent duration: .... Descent duration: ....

Total time: [   ]

Total distance covered:..

Companions:...

....

Local Pub: .... ☆ ☆ ☆ ☆ ☆

Weather conditions:..

....

Difficulty: (poor) ○ ○ ○ ○ ○ ○ ○ ○ ○ (great)

Views: (poor) ○ ○ ○ ○ ○ ○ ○ ○ ○ (great)

Enjoyment: (poor) ○ ○ ○ ○ ○ ○ ○ ○ ○ (great)

Notes/pics:

Sergeant Man

Region: Central Fells
Height: 736m / 2,415ft
OS Grid Ref: NY286088

Date: ....

Ascent start time: .... Peak time: ....

Descent start time: .... Finish time: ....

Ascent duration: .... Descent duration: ....

Total time: [   ]

Total distance covered:...

Companions:..

....

Local Pub: .... ☆ ☆ ☆ ☆ ☆

Weather conditions:..

....

Difficulty: (poor) ○ ○ ○ ○ ○ ○ ○ ○ ○ (great)

Views: (poor) ○ ○ ○ ○ ○ ○ ○ ○ ○ (great)

Enjoyment: (poor) ○ ○ ○ ○ ○ ○ ○ ○ ○ (great)

Notes/pics:

High Raise (Langdale)

Region: Central Fells
Height: 762m / 2,500ft
OS Grid Ref: NY280095

Date: ....

Ascent start time: .... Peak time: ....

Descent start time: .... Finish time: ....

Ascent duration: .... Descent duration: ....

Total time: [   ]

Total distance covered:...

Companions:..

....

Local Pub: .... ☆ ☆ ☆ ☆ ☆

Weather conditions:..

....

Difficulty: (poor) ○ ○ ○ ○ ○ ○ ○ ○ ○ (great)

Views: (poor) ○ ○ ○ ○ ○ ○ ○ ○ ○ (great)

Enjoyment: (poor) ○ ○ ○ ○ ○ ○ ○ ○ ○ (great)

Notes/pics:

Arnison Crag

Region: Eastern Fells
Height: 433m / 1,421ft
OS Grid Ref: NY393149

Date: ....

Ascent start time: .... Peak time: ....

Descent start time: .... Finish time: ....

Ascent duration: .... Descent duration: ....

Total time: [　　　　　　　]

Total distance covered:..

Companions:..

....

Local Pub: .... ☆☆☆☆☆

Weather conditions:..

....

Difficulty: (poor) ○ ○ ○ ○ ○ ○ ○ ○ ○ ○ (great)

Views: (poor) ○ ○ ○ ○ ○ ○ ○ ○ ○ ○ (great)

Enjoyment: (poor) ○ ○ ○ ○ ○ ○ ○ ○ ○ ○ (great)

Notes/pics:

Glenridding Dodd

Region: Eastern Fells
Height: 442m / 1,450ft
OS Grid Ref: NY380175

Date: ....

Ascent start time: .... Peak time: ....

Descent start time: .... Finish time: ....

Ascent duration: .... Descent duration: ....

Total time: [   ]

Total distance covered:..

Companions:...

....

Local Pub: .... ☆☆☆☆☆

Weather conditions:..

....

Difficulty: (poor) ○ ○ ○ ○ ○ ○ ○ ○ ○ (great)

Views: (poor) ○ ○ ○ ○ ○ ○ ○ ○ ○ (great)

Enjoyment: (poor) ○ ○ ○ ○ ○ ○ ○ ○ ○ (great)

Notes/pics:

Nab Scar

Region: Eastern Fells
Height: 450m / 1,476ft
OS Grid Ref: NY355072

Date: ....

Ascent start time: .... Peak time: ....

Descent start time: .... Finish time: ....

Ascent duration: .... Descent duration: ....

Total time: [   ]

Total distance covered:...

Companions:...

....

Local Pub: .... ☆ ☆ ☆ ☆ ☆

Weather conditions:...

....

Difficulty: (poor) ○ ○ ○ ○ ○ ○ ○ ○ ○ (great)

Views: (poor) ○ ○ ○ ○ ○ ○ ○ ○ ○ (great)

Enjoyment: (poor) ○ ○ ○ ○ ○ ○ ○ ○ ○ (great)

Notes/pics:

Gowbarrow Fell

Region: Eastern Fells
Height: 481m / 1,579ft
OS Grid Ref: NY407218

Date: ....

Ascent start time: .... Peak time: ....

Descent start time: .... Finish time: ....

Ascent duration: .... Descent duration: ....

Total time: [   ]

Total distance covered:...

Companions:...

....

Local Pub: .... ☆☆☆☆☆

Weather conditions:...

....

Difficulty: (poor) ⦿ ⦿ ⦿ ⦿ ⦿ ⦿ ⦿ ⦿ ⦿ (great)

Views: (poor) ⦿ ⦿ ⦿ ⦿ ⦿ ⦿ ⦿ ⦿ ⦿ (great)

Enjoyment: (poor) ⦿ ⦿ ⦿ ⦿ ⦿ ⦿ ⦿ ⦿ ⦿ (great)

Notes/pics:

Stone Arthur

Region: Eastern Fells
Height: 504m / 1,654ft
OS Grid Ref: NY347092

Date: ....

Ascent start time: .... Peak time: ....

Descent start time: .... Finish time: ....

Ascent duration: .... Descent duration: ....

Total time: [   ]

Total distance covered:...

Companions:..

....

Local Pub: .... ☆☆☆☆☆

Weather conditions:...

....

Difficulty: (poor) ○ ○ ○ ○ ○ ○ ○ ○ ○ (great)

Views: (poor) ○ ○ ○ ○ ○ ○ ○ ○ ○ (great)

Enjoyment: (poor) ○ ○ ○ ○ ○ ○ ○ ○ ○ (great)

Notes/pics:

Little Mell Fell

Region: Eastern Fells
Height: 505m / 1,657ft
OS Grid Ref: NY423240

Date: ....

Ascent start time: .... Peak time: ....

Descent start time: .... Finish time: ....

Ascent duration: .... Descent duration: ....

Total time: [   ]

Total distance covered:...

Companions:...

....

Local Pub: .... ☆ ☆ ☆ ☆ ☆

Weather conditions:..

....

Difficulty: (poor) ○ ○ ○ ○ ○ ○ ○ ○ ○ (great)

Views: (poor) ○ ○ ○ ○ ○ ○ ○ ○ ○ (great)

Enjoyment: (poor) ○ ○ ○ ○ ○ ○ ○ ○ ○ (great)

Notes/pics:

Low Pike

Region: Eastern Fells
Height: 508m / 1,667ft
OS Grid Ref: NY373078

Date: ....

Ascent start time: .... Peak time: ....

Descent start time: .... Finish time: ....

Ascent duration: .... Descent duration: ....

Total time: [   ]

Total distance covered: ....

Companions: ....

....

Local Pub: .... ☆ ☆ ☆ ☆ ☆

Weather conditions: ....

....

Difficulty: (poor) ○ ○ ○ ○ ○ ○ ○ ○ ○ (great)

Views: (poor) ○ ○ ○ ○ ○ ○ ○ ○ ○ (great)

Enjoyment: (poor) ○ ○ ○ ○ ○ ○ ○ ○ ○ (great)

Notes/pics:

High Hartsop Dodd

Region: Eastern Fells
Height: 519m / 1,703ft
OS Grid Ref: NY393107

Date: ....

Ascent start time: .... Peak time: ....

Descent start time: .... Finish time: ....

Ascent duration: .... Descent duration: ....

Total time: [   ]

Total distance covered:...

Companions:..

....

Local Pub: .... ☆☆☆☆☆

Weather conditions:..

....

Difficulty: (poor) ○ ○ ○ ○ ○ ○ ○ ○ ○ (great)

Views: (poor) ○ ○ ○ ○ ○ ○ ○ ○ ○ (great)

Enjoyment: (poor) ○ ○ ○ ○ ○ ○ ○ ○ ○ (great)

Notes/pics:

Great Mell Fell

Region: Eastern Fells
Height: 537m / 1,762ft
OS Grid Ref: NY396253

Date: ....

Ascent start time: .... Peak time: ....

Descent start time: .... Finish time: ....

Ascent duration: .... Descent duration: ....

Total time: [   ]

Total distance covered:...

Companions:...

....

Local Pub: .... ☆☆☆☆☆

Weather conditions:..

....

Difficulty: (poor) ○ ○ ○ ○ ○ ○ ○ ○ ○ ○ (great)

Views: (poor) ○ ○ ○ ○ ○ ○ ○ ○ ○ ○ (great)

Enjoyment: (poor) ○ ○ ○ ○ ○ ○ ○ ○ ○ ○ (great)

Notes/pics:

Hartsop above How

Region: Eastern Fells
Height: 581m / 1,906ft
OS Grid Ref: NY383120

Date: ....

Ascent start time: .... Peak time: ....

Descent start time: .... Finish time: ....

Ascent duration: .... Descent duration: ....

Total time: [   ]

Total distance covered: ....

Companions: ....

....

Local Pub: .... ☆ ☆ ☆ ☆ ☆

Weather conditions: ....

....

Difficulty: (poor) ○ ○ ○ ○ ○ ○ ○ ○ ○ ○ (great)

Views: (poor) ○ ○ ○ ○ ○ ○ ○ ○ ○ ○ (great)

Enjoyment: (poor) ○ ○ ○ ○ ○ ○ ○ ○ ○ ○ (great)

Notes/pics:

Heron Pike (Rydal)
Region: Eastern Fells
Height: 612m / 2,008ft
OS Grid Ref: NY355083

Date: ....

Ascent start time: .... Peak time: ....

Descent start time: .... Finish time: ....

Ascent duration: .... Descent duration: ....

Total time: [   ]

Total distance covered:...

Companions:...

....

Local Pub: .... ☆☆☆☆☆

Weather conditions:...

....

Difficulty: (poor) ○ ○ ○ ○ ○ ○ ○ ○ ○ (great)

Views: (poor) ○ ○ ○ ○ ○ ○ ○ ○ ○ (great)

Enjoyment: (poor) ○ ○ ○ ○ ○ ○ ○ ○ ○ (great)

Notes/pics:

Birks

Region: Eastern Fells
Height: 622m / 2,041ft
OS Grid Ref: NY380143

Date: ....

Ascent start time: .... Peak time: ....

Descent start time: .... Finish time: ....

Ascent duration: .... Descent duration: ....

Total time: [   ]

Total distance covered:...

Companions:..

....

Local Pub: .... ☆☆☆☆☆

Weather conditions:..

....

Difficulty: (poor) ○ ○ ○ ○ ○ ○ ○ ○ ○ (great)

Views: (poor) ○ ○ ○ ○ ○ ○ ○ ○ ○ (great)

Enjoyment: (poor) ○ ○ ○ ○ ○ ○ ○ ○ ○ (great)

Notes/pics:

Little Hart Crag (West Top)

Region: Eastern Fells
Height: 637m / 2,090ft
OS Grid Ref: NY387100

Date: ....

Ascent start time: .... Peak time: ....

Descent start time: .... Finish time: ....

Ascent duration: .... Descent duration: ....

Total time: [   ]

Total distance covered:..

Companions:...

....

Local Pub: .... ☆ ☆ ☆ ☆ ☆

Weather conditions:...

....

Difficulty: (poor) ○ ○ ○ ○ ○ ○ ○ ○ ○ ○ (great)

Views: (poor) ○ ○ ○ ○ ○ ○ ○ ○ ○ ○ (great)

Enjoyment: (poor) ○ ○ ○ ○ ○ ○ ○ ○ ○ ○ (great)

Notes/pics:

Middle Dodd

Region: Eastern Fells
Height: 654m / 2,146ft
OS Grid Ref: NY397095

Date: ....

Ascent start time: .... Peak time: ....

Descent start time: .... Finish time: ....

Ascent duration: .... Descent duration: ....

Total time: [   ]

Total distance covered:..

Companions:..
....

Local Pub: .... ☆ ☆ ☆ ☆ ☆

Weather conditions:..
....

Difficulty: (poor) ○ ○ ○ ○ ○ ○ ○ ○ ○ (great)

Views: (poor) ○ ○ ○ ○ ○ ○ ○ ○ ○ (great)

Enjoyment: (poor) ○ ○ ○ ○ ○ ○ ○ ○ ○ (great)

Notes/pics:

High Pike (Scandale)

Region: Eastern Fells
Height: 656m / 2,152ft
OS Grid Ref: NY374088

Date: ....

Ascent start time: .... Peak time: ....

Descent start time: .... Finish time: ....

Ascent duration: .... Descent duration: ....

Total time: [   ]

Total distance covered:...

Companions:...

....

Local Pub: .... ☆ ☆ ☆ ☆ ☆

Weather conditions:..

....

Difficulty: (poor) ○ ○ ○ ○ ○ ○ ○ ○ ○ ○ (great)

Views: (poor) ○ ○ ○ ○ ○ ○ ○ ○ ○ ○ (great)

Enjoyment: (poor) ○ ○ ○ ○ ○ ○ ○ ○ ○ ○ (great)

Notes/pics:

Sheffield Pike

Region: Eastern Fells
Height: 675m / 2,215ft
OS Grid Ref: NY369181

Date: ....

Ascent start time: .... Peak time: ....

Descent start time: .... Finish time: ....

Ascent duration: .... Descent duration: ....

Total time: [   ]

Total distance covered:..

Companions:..

....

Local Pub: .... ☆ ☆ ☆ ☆ ☆

Weather conditions:...

....

Difficulty: (poor) ○ ○ ○ ○ ○ ○ ○ ○ ○ (great)

Views: (poor) ○ ○ ○ ○ ○ ○ ○ ○ ○ (great)

Enjoyment: (poor) ○ ○ ○ ○ ○ ○ ○ ○ ○ (great)

Notes/pics:

Birkhouse Moor

Region: Eastern Fells
Height: 718m / 2,356ft
OS Grid Ref: NY363159

Date: ....

Ascent start time: .... Peak time: ....

Descent start time: .... Finish time: ....

Ascent duration: .... Descent duration: ....

Total time: [   ]

Total distance covered:...

Companions:...
....

Local Pub: .... ☆ ☆ ☆ ☆ ☆

Weather conditions:...
....

Difficulty: (poor) O O O O O O O O O (great)

Views: (poor) O O O O O O O O O (great)

Enjoyment: (poor) O O O O O O O O O (great)

Notes/pics:

Clough Head

Region: Eastern Fells
Height: 726m / 2,382ft
OS Grid Ref: NY333225

Date: ....

Ascent start time: .... Peak time: ....

Descent start time: .... Finish time: ....

Ascent duration: .... Descent duration: ....

Total time: [   ]

Total distance covered:..

Companions:..

....

Local Pub: .... ☆ ☆ ☆ ☆ ☆

Weather conditions:...

....

Difficulty: (poor) ○ ○ ○ ○ ○ ○ ○ ○ ○ (great)

Views: (poor) ○ ○ ○ ○ ○ ○ ○ ○ ○ (great)

Enjoyment: (poor) ○ ○ ○ ○ ○ ○ ○ ○ ○ (great)

Notes/pics:

Seat Sandal

Region: Eastern Fells
Height: 737m / 2,417ft
OS Grid Ref: NY344115

Date: ....

Ascent start time: .... Peak time: ....

Descent start time: .... Finish time: ....

Ascent duration: .... Descent duration: ....

Total time: [ ]

Total distance covered:..

Companions:...

....

Local Pub: .... ☆ ☆ ☆ ☆ ☆

Weather conditions:..

....

Difficulty: (poor) ○ ○ ○ ○ ○ ○ ○ ○ ○ ○ (great)

Views: (poor) ○ ○ ○ ○ ○ ○ ○ ○ ○ ○ (great)

Enjoyment: (poor) ○ ○ ○ ○ ○ ○ ○ ○ ○ ○ (great)

Notes/pics:

Hart Side

Region: Eastern Fells
Height: 756m / 2,480ft
OS Grid Ref: NY359197

Date: ....

Ascent start time: .... Peak time: ....

Descent start time: .... Finish time: ....

Ascent duration: .... Descent duration: ....

Total time: [   ]

Total distance covered:..

Companions:...

....

Local Pub: .... ☆ ☆ ☆ ☆ ☆

Weather conditions:...

....

Difficulty: (poor) ○ ○ ○ ○ ○ ○ ○ ○ ○ (great)

Views: (poor) ○ ○ ○ ○ ○ ○ ○ ○ ○ (great)

Enjoyment: (poor) ○ ○ ○ ○ ○ ○ ○ ○ ○ (great)

Notes/pics:

Great Rigg

Region: Eastern Fells
Height: 766m / 2,513ft
OS Grid Ref: NY355104

Date: ....

Ascent start time: .... Peak time: ....

Descent start time: .... Finish time: ....

Ascent duration: .... Descent duration: ....

Total time:

Total distance covered:...

Companions:...

....

Local Pub: .... ☆☆☆☆☆

Weather conditions:..

....

Difficulty: (poor) ○ ○ ○ ○ ○ ○ ○ ○ ○ ○ (great)

Views: (poor) ○ ○ ○ ○ ○ ○ ○ ○ ○ ○ (great)

Enjoyment: (poor) ○ ○ ○ ○ ○ ○ ○ ○ ○ ○ (great)

Notes/pics:

Red Screes

Region: Eastern Fells
Height: 776m / 2,546ft
OS Grid Ref: NY396087

Date: ....

Ascent start time: .... Peak time: ....

Descent start time: .... Finish time: ....

Ascent duration: .... Descent duration: ....

Total time: [ ]

Total distance covered:...

Companions:...

....

Local Pub: .... ☆ ☆ ☆ ☆ ☆

Weather conditions:...

....

Difficulty: (poor) ○ ○ ○ ○ ○ ○ ○ ○ ○ (great)

Views: (poor) ○ ○ ○ ○ ○ ○ ○ ○ ○ (great)

Enjoyment: (poor) ○ ○ ○ ○ ○ ○ ○ ○ ○ (great)

Notes/pics:

Watson's Dodd
Region: Eastern Fells
Height: 789m / 2,589ft
OS Grid Ref: NY335195

Date: ....

Ascent start time: .... Peak time: ....

Descent start time: .... Finish time: ....

Ascent duration: .... Descent duration: ....

Total time: [   ]

Total distance covered:..

Companions:..

....

Local Pub: .... ☆☆☆☆☆

Weather conditions:..

....

Difficulty: (poor) ○ ○ ○ ○ ○ ○ ○ ○ ○ (great)

Views: (poor) ○ ○ ○ ○ ○ ○ ○ ○ ○ (great)

Enjoyment: (poor) ○ ○ ○ ○ ○ ○ ○ ○ ○ (great)

Notes/pics:

Dove Crag

Region: Eastern Fells
Height: 792m / 2,598ft
OS Grid Ref: NY374104

Date: ....

Ascent start time: .... Peak time: ....

Descent start time: .... Finish time: ....

Ascent duration: .... Descent duration: ....

Total time: [   ]

Total distance covered:..

Companions:...

....

Local Pub: .... ☆☆☆☆☆

Weather conditions:..

....

Difficulty: (poor) ○ ○ ○ ○ ○ ○ ○ ○ ○ ○ (great)

Views: (poor) ○ ○ ○ ○ ○ ○ ○ ○ ○ ○ (great)

Enjoyment: (poor) ○ ○ ○ ○ ○ ○ ○ ○ ○ ○ (great)

Notes/pics:

Hart Crag

Region: Eastern Fells
Height: 822m / 2,697ft
OS Grid Ref: NY369112

Date: ....

Ascent start time: .... Peak time: ....

Descent start time: .... Finish time: ....

Ascent duration: .... Descent duration: ....

Total time: [ ]

Total distance covered:...

Companions:..

....

Local Pub: .... ☆ ☆ ☆ ☆ ☆

Weather conditions:...

....

Difficulty: (poor) ○ ○ ○ ○ ○ ○ ○ ○ ○ (great)

Views: (poor) ○ ○ ○ ○ ○ ○ ○ ○ ○ (great)

Enjoyment: (poor) ○ ○ ○ ○ ○ ○ ○ ○ ○ (great)

Notes/pics:

St Sunday Crag

Region: Eastern Fells
Height: 841m / 2,759ft
OS Grid Ref: NY369133

Date: ....

Ascent start time: .... Peak time: ....

Descent start time: .... Finish time: ....

Ascent duration: .... Descent duration: ....

Total time: [   ]

Total distance covered:..

Companions:..

....

Local Pub: .... ☆ ☆ ☆ ☆ ☆

Weather conditions:..

....

Difficulty: (poor) ○ ○ ○ ○ ○ ○ ○ ○ ○ ○ (great)

Views: (poor) ○ ○ ○ ○ ○ ○ ○ ○ ○ ○ (great)

Enjoyment: (poor) ○ ○ ○ ○ ○ ○ ○ ○ ○ ○ (great)

Notes/pics:

Stybarrow Dodd

Region: Eastern Fells
Height: 843m / 2,766ft
OS Grid Ref: NY343189

Date: ....

Ascent start time: .... Peak time: ....

Descent start time: .... Finish time: ....

Ascent duration: .... Descent duration: ....

Total time: [ ]

Total distance covered:..

Companions:..

....

Local Pub: .... ☆☆☆☆☆

Weather conditions:..

....

Difficulty: (poor) ○ ○ ○ ○ ○ ○ ○ ○ ○ (great)

Views: (poor) ○ ○ ○ ○ ○ ○ ○ ○ ○ (great)

Enjoyment: (poor) ○ ○ ○ ○ ○ ○ ○ ○ ○ (great)

Notes/pics:

Great Dodd

Region: Eastern Fells
Height: 857m / 2,812ft
OS Grid Ref: NY342205

Date: ....

Ascent start time: .... Peak time: ....

Descent start time: .... Finish time: ....

Ascent duration: .... Descent duration: ....

Total time: [   ]

Total distance covered:...

Companions:...

....

Local Pub: .... ☆☆☆☆☆

Weather conditions:..

....

Difficulty: (poor) ⭘ ⭘ ⭘ ⭘ ⭘ ⭘ ⭘ ⭘ ⭘ (great)

Views: (poor) ⭘ ⭘ ⭘ ⭘ ⭘ ⭘ ⭘ ⭘ ⭘ (great)

Enjoyment: (poor) ⭘ ⭘ ⭘ ⭘ ⭘ ⭘ ⭘ ⭘ ⭘ (great)

Notes/pics:

Dollywaggon Pike

Region: Eastern Fells
Height: 858m / 2,815ft
OS Grid Ref: NY346130

Date: ....

Ascent start time: .... Peak time: ....

Descent start time: .... Finish time: ....

Ascent duration: .... Descent duration: ....

Total time: [   ]

Total distance covered:..

Companions:..

....

Local Pub: .... ☆☆☆☆☆

Weather conditions:..

....

Difficulty: (poor) ○ ○ ○ ○ ○ ○ ○ ○ ○ (great)

Views: (poor) ○ ○ ○ ○ ○ ○ ○ ○ ○ (great)

Enjoyment: (poor) ○ ○ ○ ○ ○ ○ ○ ○ ○ (great)

Notes/pics:

White Side

Region: Eastern Fells
Height: 863m / 2,831ft
OS Grid Ref: NY337166

Date: ....

Ascent start time: .... Peak time: ....

Descent start time: .... Finish time: ....

Ascent duration: .... Descent duration: ....

Total time: [   ]

Total distance covered:...

Companions:...

....

Local Pub: .... ☆ ☆ ☆ ☆ ☆

Weather conditions:...

....

Difficulty: (poor) ○ ○ ○ ○ ○ ○ ○ ○ ○ (great)

Views: (poor) ○ ○ ○ ○ ○ ○ ○ ○ ○ (great)

Enjoyment: (poor) ○ ○ ○ ○ ○ ○ ○ ○ ○ (great)

Notes/pics:

Fairfield

Region: Eastern Fells
Height: 873m / 2,864ft
OS Grid Ref: NY358117

Date: ....

Ascent start time: .... Peak time: ....

Descent start time: .... Finish time: ....

Ascent duration: .... Descent duration: ....

Total time: [   ]

Total distance covered:...

Companions:..

....

Local Pub: .... ☆☆☆☆☆

Weather conditions:..

....

Difficulty: (poor) ○ ○ ○ ○ ○ ○ ○ ○ ○ ○ (great)

Views: (poor) ○ ○ ○ ○ ○ ○ ○ ○ ○ ○ (great)

Enjoyment: (poor) ○ ○ ○ ○ ○ ○ ○ ○ ○ ○ (great)

Notes/pics:

Raise

Region: Eastern Fells
Height: 883m / 2,897ft
OS Grid Ref: NY342174

Date: ....

Ascent start time: .... Peak time: ....

Descent start time: .... Finish time: ....

Ascent duration: .... Descent duration: ....

Total time: [   ]

Total distance covered:...

Companions:...

....

Local Pub: .... ☆☆☆☆☆

Weather conditions:...

....

Difficulty: (poor) ○ ○ ○ ○ ○ ○ ○ ○ ○ ○ (great)

Views: (poor) ○ ○ ○ ○ ○ ○ ○ ○ ○ ○ (great)

Enjoyment: (poor) ○ ○ ○ ○ ○ ○ ○ ○ ○ ○ (great)

Notes/pics:

Catstye cam

Region: Eastern Fells
Height: 890m / 2,920ft
OS Grid Ref: NY348158

Date: ....

Ascent start time: .... Peak time: ....

Descent start time: .... Finish time: ....

Ascent duration: .... Descent duration: ....

Total time: [   ]

Total distance covered:..

Companions:...

....

Local Pub: .... ☆☆☆☆☆

Weather conditions:...

....

Difficulty: (poor) ○○○○○○○○○ (great)

Views: (poor) ○○○○○○○○○ (great)

Enjoyment: (poor) ○○○○○○○○○ (great)

Notes/pics:

Nethermost Pike

Region: Eastern Fells
Height: 891m / 2,923ft
OS Grid Ref: NY343142

Date: ....

Ascent start time: .... Peak time: ....

Descent start time: .... Finish time: ....

Ascent duration: .... Descent duration: ....

Total time: [   ]

Total distance covered:..

Companions:..

....

Local Pub: .... ☆ ☆ ☆ ☆ ☆

Weather conditions:..

....

Difficulty: (poor) ⃝ ⃝ ⃝ ⃝ ⃝ ⃝ ⃝ ⃝ ⃝ ⃝ (great)

Views: (poor) ⃝ ⃝ ⃝ ⃝ ⃝ ⃝ ⃝ ⃝ ⃝ ⃝ (great)

Enjoyment: (poor) ⃝ ⃝ ⃝ ⃝ ⃝ ⃝ ⃝ ⃝ ⃝ ⃝ (great)

Notes/pics:

Helvellyn
Region: Eastern Fells
Height: 950m / 3,117ft
OS Grid Ref: NY342151

Date: ....

Ascent start time: .... Peak time: ....

Descent start time: .... Finish time: ....

Ascent duration: .... Descent duration: ....

Total time: [   ]

Total distance covered:..

Companions:..

....

Local Pub: .... ☆☆☆☆☆

Weather conditions:...

....

Difficulty: (poor) ○ ○ ○ ○ ○ ○ ○ ○ ○ (great)

Views: (poor) ○ ○ ○ ○ ○ ○ ○ ○ ○ (great)

Enjoyment: (poor) ○ ○ ○ ○ ○ ○ ○ ○ ○ (great)

Notes/pics:

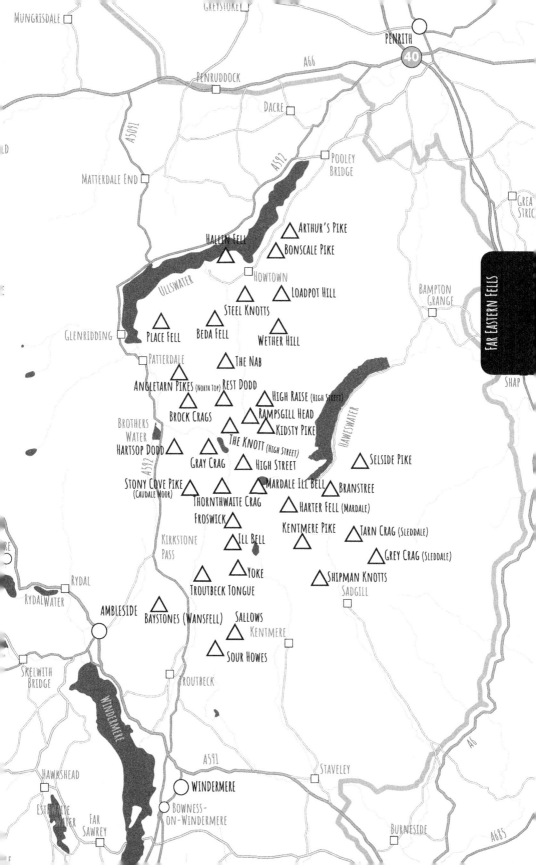

MUNGRISDALE

GREYSTOKE

PENRITH

40

A66

PENRUDDOCK

DACRE

A592

POOLEY BRIDGE

MATTERDALE END

A5091

GREAT STRIC

Arthur's Pike

Bonscale Pike

Hallin Fell

Howtown

Ullswater

Loadpot Hill

BAMPTON GRANGE

Steel Knotts

Place Fell

Beda Fell

Wether Hill

SHAP

GLENRIDDING

PATTERDALE

The Nab

Angletarn Pikes (North Top)

Rest Dodd

High Raise (High Street)

Brock Crags

Rampsgill Head

Kidsty Pike

Hawswater

BROTHERS WATER

The Knott (High Street)

Hartsop Dodd

Gray Crag

High Street

Selside Pike

A592

Stony Cove Pike (Caudale Moor)

Mardale Ill Bell

Branstree

Thornthwaite Crag

Harter Fell (Mardale)

Froswick

Kentmere Pike

Tarn Crag (Sleddale)

KIRKSTONE PASS

Ill Bell

Grey Crag (Sleddale)

RYDAL

Yoke

Shipman Knotts

SADGILL

RYDAL WATER

Troutbeck Tongue

AMBLESIDE

Baystones (Wansfell)

Sallows

KENTMERE

SKELWITH BRIDGE

Sour Howes

TROUTBECK

WINDERMERE

HAWKSHEAD

A591

STAVELEY

ESTHWAITE WATER

FAR SAWREY

WINDERMERE

BOWNESS-ON-WINDERMERE

BURNESIDE

A6

A685

Troutbeck Tongue

Region: Far Eastern Fells
Height: 364m / 1,194ft
OS Grid Ref: NY422064

Date: ....

Ascent start time: .... Peak time: ....

Descent start time: .... Finish time: ....

Ascent duration: .... Descent duration: ....

Total time: [   ]

Total distance covered:...

Companions:...

....

Local Pub: .... ☆☆☆☆☆

Weather conditions:...

....

Difficulty: (poor) ○ ○ ○ ○ ○ ○ ○ ○ ○ (great)

Views: (poor) ○ ○ ○ ○ ○ ○ ○ ○ ○ (great)

Enjoyment: (poor) ○ ○ ○ ○ ○ ○ ○ ○ ○ (great)

Notes/pics:

Hallin Fell

Region: Far Eastern Fells
Height: 388m / 1,273ft
OS Grid Ref: NY433198

Date: ....

Ascent start time: .... Peak time: ....

Descent start time: .... Finish time: ....

Ascent duration: .... Descent duration: ....

Total time: [   ]

Total distance covered:...

Companions:..
....

Local Pub: .... ☆ ☆ ☆ ☆ ☆

Weather conditions:...
....

Difficulty: (poor) ○ ○ ○ ○ ○ ○ ○ ○ ○ (great)

Views: (poor) ○ ○ ○ ○ ○ ○ ○ ○ ○ (great)

Enjoyment: (poor) ○ ○ ○ ○ ○ ○ ○ ○ ○ (great)

Notes/pics:

Steel Knotts
Region: Far Eastern Fells
Height: 432m / 1,417ft
OS Grid Ref: NY440181

Date: ....

Ascent start time: .... Peak time: ....

Descent start time: .... Finish time: ....

Ascent duration: .... Descent duration: ....

Total time: [ ]

Total distance covered: ....

Companions: ....

....

Local Pub: .... ☆☆☆☆☆

Weather conditions: ....

....

Difficulty: (poor) ○ ○ ○ ○ ○ ○ ○ ○ ○ (great)

Views: (poor) ○ ○ ○ ○ ○ ○ ○ ○ ○ (great)

Enjoyment: (poor) ○ ○ ○ ○ ○ ○ ○ ○ ○ (great)

Notes/pics:

Sour Howes

Region: Far Eastern Fells
Height: 483m / 1,585ft
OS Grid Ref: NY427032

Date: ....

Ascent start time: .... Peak time: ....

Descent start time: .... Finish time: ....

Ascent duration: .... Descent duration: ....

Total time: [   ]

Total distance covered:..

Companions:..

....

Local Pub: .... ☆ ☆ ☆ ☆ ☆

Weather conditions:...

....

Difficulty: (poor) ○ ○ ○ ○ ○ ○ ○ ○ ○ (great)

Views: (poor) ○ ○ ○ ○ ○ ○ ○ ○ ○ (great)

Enjoyment: (poor) ○ ○ ○ ○ ○ ○ ○ ○ ○ (great)

Notes/pics:

Baystones (Wansfell)

Region: Far Eastern Fells
Height: 487m / 1,597ft
OS Grid Ref: NY403051

Date: ....

Ascent start time: .... Peak time: ....

Descent start time: .... Finish time: ....

Ascent duration: .... Descent duration: ....

Total time: [   ]

Total distance covered:...

Companions:...

....

Local Pub: .... ☆☆☆☆☆

Weather conditions:..

....

Difficulty: (poor) ○ ○ ○ ○ ○ ○ ○ ○ ○ (great)

Views: (poor) ○ ○ ○ ○ ○ ○ ○ ○ ○ (great)

Enjoyment: (poor) ○ ○ ○ ○ ○ ○ ○ ○ ○ (great)

Notes/pics:

Beda Fell (Beda Head)

Region: Far Eastern Fells
Height: 509m / 1,670ft
OS Grid Ref: NY428171

Date: ....

Ascent start time: .... Peak time: ....

Descent start time: .... Finish time: ....

Ascent duration: .... Descent duration: ....

Total time: [   ]

Total distance covered:..

Companions:...

....

Local Pub: .... ☆☆☆☆☆

Weather conditions:..

....

Difficulty: (poor) ○ ○ ○ ○ ○ ○ ○ ○ ○ (great)

Views: (poor) ○ ○ ○ ○ ○ ○ ○ ○ ○ (great)

Enjoyment: (poor) ○ ○ ○ ○ ○ ○ ○ ○ ○ (great)

Notes/pics:

Sallows

Region: Far Eastern Fells
Height: 516m / 1,693ft
OS Grid Ref: NY436039

Date: ....

Ascent start time: .... Peak time: ....

Descent start time: .... Finish time: ....

Ascent duration: .... Descent duration: ....

Total time: [   ]

Total distance covered:...

Companions:...

....

Local Pub: .... ☆ ☆ ☆ ☆ ☆

Weather conditions:...

....

Difficulty: (poor) O O O O O O O O O (great)

Views: (poor) O O O O O O O O O (great)

Enjoyment: (poor) O O O O O O O O O (great)

Notes/pics:

Bonscale Pike

Region: Far Eastern Fells
Height: 524m / 1,719ft
OS Grid Ref: NY453200

Date: ....

Ascent start time: .... Peak time: ....

Descent start time: .... Finish time: ....

Ascent duration: .... Descent duration: ....

Total time: [   ]

Total distance covered:...

Companions:...
....

Local Pub: .... ☆☆☆☆☆

Weather conditions:...
....

Difficulty: (poor) ○ ○ ○ ○ ○ ○ ○ ○ ○ (great)

Views: (poor) ○ ○ ○ ○ ○ ○ ○ ○ ○ (great)

Enjoyment: (poor) ○ ○ ○ ○ ○ ○ ○ ○ ○ (great)

Notes/pics:

Arthur's Pike

Region: Far Eastern Fells
Height: 533m / 1,749ft
OS Grid Ref: NY460206

Date: ....

Ascent start time: .... Peak time: ....

Descent start time: .... Finish time: ....

Ascent duration: .... Descent duration: ....

Total time: [ ]

Total distance covered:...

Companions:...

....

Local Pub: .... ☆ ☆ ☆ ☆ ☆

Weather conditions:..

....

Difficulty: (poor) ○ ○ ○ ○ ○ ○ ○ ○ ○ (great)

Views: (poor) ○ ○ ○ ○ ○ ○ ○ ○ ○ (great)

Enjoyment: (poor) ○ ○ ○ ○ ○ ○ ○ ○ ○ (great)

Notes/pics:

Brock Crags

Region: Far Eastern Fells
Height: 561m / 1,841ft
OS Grid Ref: NY416136

Date: ....

Ascent start time: .... Peak time: ....

Descent start time: .... Finish time: ....

Ascent duration: .... Descent duration: ....

Total time: [   ]

Total distance covered:..

Companions:...

....

Local Pub: .... ☆ ☆ ☆ ☆ ☆

Weather conditions:..

....

Difficulty: (poor) ○ ○ ○ ○ ○ ○ ○ ○ ○ ○ (great)

Views: (poor) ○ ○ ○ ○ ○ ○ ○ ○ ○ ○ (great)

Enjoyment: (poor) ○ ○ ○ ○ ○ ○ ○ ○ ○ ○ (great)

Notes/pics:

Angletarn Pikes (North Top)

Region: Far Eastern Fells
Height: 567m / 1,860ft
OS Grid Ref: NY413148

Date: ....

Ascent start time: .... Peak time: ....

Descent start time: .... Finish time: ....

Ascent duration: .... Descent duration: ....

Total time: [   ]

Total distance covered:...

Companions:...

....

Local Pub: .... ☆ ☆ ☆ ☆ ☆

Weather conditions:..

....

Difficulty: (poor) ○ ○ ○ ○ ○ ○ ○ ○ ○ ○ (great)

Views: (poor) ○ ○ ○ ○ ○ ○ ○ ○ ○ ○ (great)

Enjoyment: (poor) ○ ○ ○ ○ ○ ○ ○ ○ ○ ○ (great)

Notes/pics:

The Nab

Region: Far Eastern Fells
Height: 576m / 1,890ft
OS Grid Ref: NY434151

Date: ....

Ascent start time: .... Peak time: ....

Descent start time: .... Finish time: ....

Ascent duration: .... Descent duration: ....

Total time: [   ]

Total distance covered:...

Companions:..

....

Local Pub: .... ☆ ☆ ☆ ☆ ☆

Weather conditions:..

....

Difficulty: (poor) ○ ○ ○ ○ ○ ○ ○ ○ ○ (great)

Views: (poor) ○ ○ ○ ○ ○ ○ ○ ○ ○ (great)

Enjoyment: (poor) ○ ○ ○ ○ ○ ○ ○ ○ ○ (great)

Notes/pics:

Shipman Knotts
Region: Far Eastern Fells
Height: 587m / 1,926ft
OS Grid Ref: NY472062

Date: ....

Ascent start time: .... Peak time: ....

Descent start time: .... Finish time: ....

Ascent duration: .... Descent duration: ....

Total time: [   ]

Total distance covered:..

Companions:..

....

Local Pub: .... ☆☆☆☆☆

Weather conditions:..

....

Difficulty: (poor) ○ ○ ○ ○ ○ ○ ○ ○ ○ ○ (great)

Views: (poor) ○ ○ ○ ○ ○ ○ ○ ○ ○ ○ (great)

Enjoyment: (poor) ○ ○ ○ ○ ○ ○ ○ ○ ○ ○ (great)

Notes/pics:

Hartsop Dodd

Region: Far Eastern Fells
Height: 618m / 2,028ft
OS Grid Ref: NY411118

Date: ....

Ascent start time: .... Peak time: ....

Descent start time: .... Finish time: ....

Ascent duration: .... Descent duration: ....

Total time: [   ]

Total distance covered:..

Companions:...

....

Local Pub: .... ☆ ☆ ☆ ☆ ☆

Weather conditions:..

....

Difficulty: (poor) ○ ○ ○ ○ ○ ○ ○ ○ ○ (great)

Views: (poor) ○ ○ ○ ○ ○ ○ ○ ○ ○ (great)

Enjoyment: (poor) ○ ○ ○ ○ ○ ○ ○ ○ ○ (great)

Notes/pics:

Grey Crag (Sleddale)

Region: Far Eastern Fells
Height: 638m / 2,093ft
OS Grid Ref: NY497072

Date: ....

Ascent start time: .... Peak time: ....

Descent start time: .... Finish time: ....

Ascent duration: .... Descent duration: ....

Total time: [   ]

Total distance covered:...

Companions:..

....

Local Pub: .... ☆ ☆ ☆ ☆ ☆

Weather conditions:...

....

Difficulty: (poor) ○ ○ ○ ○ ○ ○ ○ ○ ○ ○ (great)

Views: (poor) ○ ○ ○ ○ ○ ○ ○ ○ ○ ○ (great)

Enjoyment: (poor) ○ ○ ○ ○ ○ ○ ○ ○ ○ ○ (great)

Notes/pics:

Selside Pike

Region: Far Eastern Fells
Height: 655m / 2,149ft
OS Grid Ref: NY490111

Date: ....

Ascent start time: .... Peak time: ....

Descent start time: .... Finish time: ....

Ascent duration: .... Descent duration: ....

Total time: [   ]

Total distance covered:...

Companions:...

....

Local Pub: .... ☆☆☆☆☆

Weather conditions:...

....

Difficulty: (poor) ○ ○ ○ ○ ○ ○ ○ ○ ○ (great)

Views: (poor) ○ ○ ○ ○ ○ ○ ○ ○ ○ (great)

Enjoyment: (poor) ○ ○ ○ ○ ○ ○ ○ ○ ○ (great)

Notes/pics:

Place Fell

Region: Far Eastern Fells
Height: 657m / 2,156ft
OS Grid Ref: NY405169

Date: ....

Ascent start time: .... Peak time: ....

Descent start time: .... Finish time: ....

Ascent duration: .... Descent duration: ....

Total time: [   ]

Total distance covered:..

Companions:..

....

Local Pub: .... ☆ ☆ ☆ ☆ ☆

Weather conditions:...

....

Difficulty: (poor) ○ ○ ○ ○ ○ ○ ○ ○ ○ ○ (great)

Views: (poor) ○ ○ ○ ○ ○ ○ ○ ○ ○ ○ (great)

Enjoyment: (poor) ○ ○ ○ ○ ○ ○ ○ ○ ○ ○ (great)

Notes/pics:

Tarn Crag (Sleddale)

Region: Far Eastern Fells
Height: 664m / 2,178ft
OS Grid Ref: NY488078

Date: ....

Ascent start time: .... Peak time: ....

Descent start time: .... Finish time: ....

Ascent duration: .... Descent duration: ....

Total time: [   ]

Total distance covered:..

Companions:...

....

Local Pub: .... ☆☆☆☆☆

Weather conditions:..

....

Difficulty: (poor) ○○○○○○○○○○ (great)

Views: (poor) ○○○○○○○○○○ (great)

Enjoyment: (poor) ○○○○○○○○○○ (great)

Notes/pics:

Loadpot Hill
Region: Far Eastern Fells
Height: 672m / 2,205ft
OS Grid Ref: NY456180

Date: ....

Ascent start time: .... Peak time: ....

Descent start time: .... Finish time: ....

Ascent duration: .... Descent duration: ....

Total time: [ ]

Total distance covered:..

Companions:..

....

Local Pub: .... ☆☆☆☆☆

Weather conditions:...

....

Difficulty: (poor) ○ ○ ○ ○ ○ ○ ○ ○ ○ (great)

Views: (poor) ○ ○ ○ ○ ○ ○ ○ ○ ○ (great)

Enjoyment: (poor) ○ ○ ○ ○ ○ ○ ○ ○ ○ (great)

Notes/pics:

Wether Hill

Region: Far Eastern Fells
Height: 671m / 2,201ft
OS Grid Ref: NY455167

Date: ....

Ascent start time: .... Peak time: ....

Descent start time: .... Finish time: ....

Ascent duration: .... Descent duration: ....

Total time: [   ]

Total distance covered:...

Companions:...

....

Local Pub: .... ☆ ☆ ☆ ☆ ☆

Weather conditions:...

....

Difficulty: (poor) ○ ○ ○ ○ ○ ○ ○ ○ ○ (great)

Views: (poor) ○ ○ ○ ○ ○ ○ ○ ○ ○ (great)

Enjoyment: (poor) ○ ○ ○ ○ ○ ○ ○ ○ ○ (great)

Notes/pics:

Rest Dodd

Region: Far Eastern Fells
Height: 696m / 2,283ft
OS Grid Ref: NY432136

Date: ....

Ascent start time: .... Peak time: ....

Descent start time: .... Finish time: ....

Ascent duration: .... Descent duration: ....

Total time: [   ]

Total distance covered:..

Companions:...

....

Local Pub: .... ☆☆☆☆☆

Weather conditions:...

....

Difficulty: (poor) ○ ○ ○ ○ ○ ○ ○ ○ ○ ○ (great)

Views: (poor) ○ ○ ○ ○ ○ ○ ○ ○ ○ ○ (great)

Enjoyment: (poor) ○ ○ ○ ○ ○ ○ ○ ○ ○ ○ (great)

Notes/pics:

Gray Crag

Region: Far Eastern Fells
Height: 699m / 2,293ft
OS Grid Ref: NY427117

Date: ....

Ascent start time: .... Peak time: ....

Descent start time: .... Finish time: ....

Ascent duration: .... Descent duration: ....

Total time: [   ]

Total distance covered:...

Companions:...

....

Local Pub: .... ☆ ☆ ☆ ☆ ☆

Weather conditions:...

....

Difficulty: (poor) ○ ○ ○ ○ ○ ○ ○ ○ ○ ○ (great)

Views: (poor) ○ ○ ○ ○ ○ ○ ○ ○ ○ ○ (great)

Enjoyment: (poor) ○ ○ ○ ○ ○ ○ ○ ○ ○ ○ (great)

Notes/pics:

Yoke

Region: Far Eastern Fells
Height: 706m / 2,316ft
OS Grid Ref: NY437067

Date: ....

Ascent start time: .... Peak time: ....

Descent start time: .... Finish time: ....

Ascent duration: .... Descent duration: ....

Total time: [   ]

Total distance covered:..

Companions:..

....

Local Pub: .... ☆ ☆ ☆ ☆ ☆

Weather conditions:..

....

Difficulty: (poor) O O O O O O O O O (great)

Views: (poor) O O O O O O O O O (great)

Enjoyment: (poor) O O O O O O O O O (great)

Notes/pics:

Branstree

Region: Far Eastern Fells
Height: 713m / 2,339ft
OS Grid Ref: NY478099

Date: ....

Ascent start time: .... Peak time: ....

Descent start time: .... Finish time: ....

Ascent duration: .... Descent duration: ....

Total time: [   ]

Total distance covered:...

Companions:..

....

Local Pub: .... ☆☆☆☆☆

Weather conditions:...

....

Difficulty: (poor) ○ ○ ○ ○ ○ ○ ○ ○ ○ (great)

Views: (poor) ○ ○ ○ ○ ○ ○ ○ ○ ○ (great)

Enjoyment: (poor) ○ ○ ○ ○ ○ ○ ○ ○ ○ (great)

Notes/pics:

Froswick

Region: Far Eastern Fells
Height: 720m / 2,362ft
OS Grid Ref: NY435085

Date: ....

Ascent start time: .... Peak time: ....

Descent start time: .... Finish time: ....

Ascent duration: .... Descent duration: ....

Total time: [   ]

Total distance covered:...

Companions:..

....

Local Pub: .... ☆ ☆ ☆ ☆ ☆

Weather conditions:..

....

Difficulty: (poor) ○ ○ ○ ○ ○ ○ ○ ○ ○ (great)

Views: (poor) ○ ○ ○ ○ ○ ○ ○ ○ ○ (great)

Enjoyment: (poor) ○ ○ ○ ○ ○ ○ ○ ○ ○ (great)

Notes/pics:

Kentmere Pike

Region: Far Eastern Fells
Height: 730m / 2,395ft
OS Grid Ref: NY465077

Date: ....

Ascent start time: .... Peak time: ....

Descent start time: .... Finish time: ....

Ascent duration: .... Descent duration: ....

Total time: [   ]

Total distance covered:..

Companions:...

....

Local Pub: .... ☆☆☆☆☆

Weather conditions:..

....

Difficulty: (poor) ○ ○ ○ ○ ○ ○ ○ ○ ○ (great)

Views: (poor) ○ ○ ○ ○ ○ ○ ○ ○ ○ (great)

Enjoyment: (poor) ○ ○ ○ ○ ○ ○ ○ ○ ○ (great)

Notes/pics:

The Knott (High Street)

Region: Far Eastern Fells
Height: 739m / 2,425ft
OS Grid Ref: NY437126

Date: ....

Ascent start time: .... Peak time: ....

Descent start time: .... Finish time: ....

Ascent duration: .... Descent duration: ....

Total time: [   ]

Total distance covered:...

Companions:..

....

Local Pub: .... ☆ ☆ ☆ ☆ ☆

Weather conditions:..

....

Difficulty: (poor) ○ ○ ○ ○ ○ ○ ○ ○ ○ ○ (great)

Views: (poor) ○ ○ ○ ○ ○ ○ ○ ○ ○ ○ (great)

Enjoyment: (poor) ○ ○ ○ ○ ○ ○ ○ ○ ○ ○ (great)

Notes/pics:

Ill Bell

Region: Far Eastern Fells
Height: 757m / 2,484ft
OS Grid Ref: NY436077

Date: ....

Ascent start time: .... Peak time: ....

Descent start time: .... Finish time: ....

Ascent duration: .... Descent duration: ....

Total time: [   ]

Total distance covered:..

Companions:...

....

Local Pub: .... ☆ ☆ ☆ ☆ ☆

Weather conditions:...

....

Difficulty: (poor) ○ ○ ○ ○ ○ ○ ○ ○ ○ (great)

Views: (poor) ○ ○ ○ ○ ○ ○ ○ ○ ○ (great)

Enjoyment: (poor) ○ ○ ○ ○ ○ ○ ○ ○ ○ (great)

Notes/pics:

Mardale III Bell
Region: Far Eastern Fells
Height: 760m / 2,493ft
OS Grid Ref: NY447101

Date: ....

Ascent start time: .... Peak time: ....

Descent start time: .... Finish time: ....

Ascent duration: .... Descent duration: ....

Total time: [   ]

Total distance covered:...

Companions:...

....

Local Pub: .... ☆ ☆ ☆ ☆ ☆

Weather conditions:..

....

Difficulty: (poor) ○ ○ ○ ○ ○ ○ ○ ○ ○ ○ (great)

Views: (poor) ○ ○ ○ ○ ○ ○ ○ ○ ○ ○ (great)

Enjoyment: (poor) ○ ○ ○ ○ ○ ○ ○ ○ ○ ○ (great)

Notes/pics:

Stony Cove Pike (Caudale Moor)

Region: Far Eastern Fells
Height: 763m / 2,503ft
OS Grid Ref: NY417100

Date: ....

Ascent start time: .... Peak time: ....

Descent start time: .... Finish time: ....

Ascent duration: .... Descent duration: ....

Total time: [   ]

Total distance covered:..

Companions:..

....

Local Pub: .... ☆ ☆ ☆ ☆ ☆

Weather conditions:..

....

Difficulty: (poor) ○ ○ ○ ○ ○ ○ ○ ○ ○ ○ (great)

Views: (poor) ○ ○ ○ ○ ○ ○ ○ ○ ○ ○ (great)

Enjoyment: (poor) ○ ○ ○ ○ ○ ○ ○ ○ ○ ○ (great)

Notes/pics:

Harter Fell (Mardale)

Region: Far Eastern Fells
Height: 779m / 2,556ft
OS Grid Ref: NY459093

Date: ....

Ascent start time: .... Peak time: ....

Descent start time: .... Finish time: ....

Ascent duration: .... Descent duration: ....

Total time: [   ]

Total distance covered:...

Companions:..

....

Local Pub: .... ☆ ☆ ☆ ☆ ☆

Weather conditions:..

....

Difficulty: (poor) ○ ○ ○ ○ ○ ○ ○ ○ ○ (great)

Views: (poor) ○ ○ ○ ○ ○ ○ ○ ○ ○ (great)

Enjoyment: (poor) ○ ○ ○ ○ ○ ○ ○ ○ ○ (great)

Notes/pics:

Kidsty Pike

Region: Far Eastern Fells
Height: 780m / 2,559ft
OS Grid Ref: NY447125

Date: ....

Ascent start time: .... Peak time: ....

Descent start time: .... Finish time: ....

Ascent duration: .... Descent duration: ....

Total time:

Total distance covered:...

Companions:...

....

Local Pub: .... ☆ ☆ ☆ ☆ ☆

Weather conditions:..

....

Difficulty: (poor) ○ ○ ○ ○ ○ ○ ○ ○ ○ (great)

Views: (poor) ○ ○ ○ ○ ○ ○ ○ ○ ○ (great)

Enjoyment: (poor) ○ ○ ○ ○ ○ ○ ○ ○ ○ (great)

Notes/pics:

Thornthwaite Crag

Region: Far Eastern Fells
Height: 784m / 2,572ft
OS Grid Ref: NY431100

Date: ....

Ascent start time: .... Peak time: ....

Descent start time: .... Finish time: ....

Ascent duration: .... Descent duration: ....

Total time: [   ]

Total distance covered:...

Companions:...

....

Local Pub: .... ☆ ☆ ☆ ☆ ☆

Weather conditions:..

....

Difficulty: (poor) ○ ○ ○ ○ ○ ○ ○ ○ ○ (great)

Views: (poor) ○ ○ ○ ○ ○ ○ ○ ○ ○ (great)

Enjoyment: (poor) ○ ○ ○ ○ ○ ○ ○ ○ ○ (great)

Notes/pics:

Rampsgill Head

Region: Far Eastern Fells
Height: 792m / 2,598ft
OS Grid Ref: NY443128

Date: ....

Ascent start time: .... Peak time: ....

Descent start time: .... Finish time: ....

Ascent duration: .... Descent duration: ....

Total time: [   ]

Total distance covered:...

Companions:..

....

Local Pub: .... ☆☆☆☆☆

Weather conditions:...

....

Difficulty: (poor) ○ ○ ○ ○ ○ ○ ○ ○ ○ ○ (great)

Views: (poor) ○ ○ ○ ○ ○ ○ ○ ○ ○ ○ (great)

Enjoyment: (poor) ○ ○ ○ ○ ○ ○ ○ ○ ○ ○ (great)

Notes/pics:

High Raise (High Street)
Region: Far Eastern Fells
Height: 802m / 2,631ft
OS Grid Ref: NY448134

Date: ....

Ascent start time: .... Peak time: ....

Descent start time: .... Finish time: ....

Ascent duration: .... Descent duration: ....

Total time: [   ]

Total distance covered:...

Companions:..

....

Local Pub: .... ☆☆☆☆☆

Weather conditions:..

....

Difficulty: (poor) ○ ○ ○ ○ ○ ○ ○ ○ ○ ○ (great)

Views: (poor) ○ ○ ○ ○ ○ ○ ○ ○ ○ ○ (great)

Enjoyment: (poor) ○ ○ ○ ○ ○ ○ ○ ○ ○ ○ (great)

Notes/pics:

High Street

Region: Far Eastern Fells
Height: 828m / 2,717ft
OS Grid Ref: NY440110

Date: ....

Ascent start time: .... Peak time: ....

Descent start time: .... Finish time: ....

Ascent duration: .... Descent duration: ....

Total time: [   ]

Total distance covered:...

Companions:...

....

Local Pub: .... ☆ ☆ ☆ ☆ ☆

Weather conditions:..

....

Difficulty: (poor) ○ ○ ○ ○ ○ ○ ○ ○ ○ (great)

Views: (poor) ○ ○ ○ ○ ○ ○ ○ ○ ○ (great)

Enjoyment: (poor) ○ ○ ○ ○ ○ ○ ○ ○ ○ (great)

Notes/pics:

BOTHEL

IREBY

A591

OVER WATER

COCKERMOUTH

BASSENTHWAITE

A66

A5086

EMBLETON

Sale Fell

Ling Fell

BASSENTHWAITE LAKE

APPLETHWAITE

Graystones

Broom Fell

Lord's Seat

Barf

Low
Lorton

B5292

Whinlatter

KESWICK

PORTINSCALE

B5289

Grisedale Pike

BRAITHWAITE

Hopegill Head

Barrow

Outerside

Whiteside (West Top)

Causey Pike

Loweswater

Crag Hill (Eel Crag)

DERWENTWATER

Grasmoor

Scar Crags

THIRLMERE

Sail

Ard Crags

Whiteless Pike

Wandope

Cat Bells

THIRLMERE

Knott Rigg

Rannerdale Knotts

CRUMMOCK WATER

Maiden Moor

BUTTERMERE

Robinson

High Spy

BUTTERMERE

Hindscarth

Castle Crag

HONISTER PASS

Dale Head

SEATOLLER

ENNERDALE WATER

SEATHWAITE

NORTH WESTERN FELLS

WASDALE
HEAD

GRASMERE

CHAPE

ELTERWATER

NETHER

WAST WATER

Castle Crag

Region: North Western Fells
Height: 290m / 951ft
OS Grid Ref: NY249159

Date: ....

Ascent start time: .... Peak time: ....

Descent start time: .... Finish time: ....

Ascent duration: .... Descent duration: ....

Total time: [   ]

Total distance covered:...

Companions:..

....

Local Pub: .... ☆ ☆ ☆ ☆ ☆

Weather conditions:..

....

Difficulty: (poor) ○ ○ ○ ○ ○ ○ ○ ○ ○ (great)

Views: (poor) ○ ○ ○ ○ ○ ○ ○ ○ ○ (great)

Enjoyment: (poor) ○ ○ ○ ○ ○ ○ ○ ○ ○ (great)

Notes/pics:

Rannerdale Knotts

Region: North Western Fells
Height: 355m / 1,165ft
OS Grid Ref: NY167182

Date: ....

Ascent start time: .... Peak time: ....

Descent start time: .... Finish time: ....

Ascent duration: .... Descent duration: ....

Total time: [   ]

Total distance covered:..

Companions:..

....

Local Pub: .... ☆ ☆ ☆ ☆ ☆

Weather conditions:..

....

Difficulty: (poor) ○ ○ ○ ○ ○ ○ ○ ○ ○ (great)

Views: (poor) ○ ○ ○ ○ ○ ○ ○ ○ ○ (great)

Enjoyment: (poor) ○ ○ ○ ○ ○ ○ ○ ○ ○ (great)

Notes/pics:

Sale Fell

Region: North Western Fells
Height: 359m / 1,178ft
OS Grid Ref: NY194296

Date: ....

Ascent start time: .... Peak time: ....

Descent start time: .... Finish time: ....

Ascent duration: .... Descent duration: ....

Total time: [   ]

Total distance covered:...

Companions:..

....

Local Pub: .... ☆☆☆☆☆

Weather conditions:..

....

Difficulty: (poor) ○ ○ ○ ○ ○ ○ ○ ○ ○ (great)

Views: (poor) ○ ○ ○ ○ ○ ○ ○ ○ ○ (great)

Enjoyment: (poor) ○ ○ ○ ○ ○ ○ ○ ○ ○ (great)

Notes/pics:

Ling Fell

Region: North Western Fells
Height: 373m / 1,224ft
OS Grid Ref: NY179285

Date: ....

Ascent start time: .... Peak time: ....

Descent start time: .... Finish time: ....

Ascent duration: .... Descent duration: ....

Total time: [   ]

Total distance covered:..

Companions:..

....

Local Pub: .... ☆ ☆ ☆ ☆ ☆

Weather conditions:..

....

Difficulty: (poor) ○ ○ ○ ○ ○ ○ ○ ○ ○ ○ (great)

Views: (poor) ○ ○ ○ ○ ○ ○ ○ ○ ○ ○ (great)

Enjoyment: (poor) ○ ○ ○ ○ ○ ○ ○ ○ ○ ○ (great)

Notes/pics:

Graystones

Region: North Western Fells
Height: 452m / 1,483ft
OS Grid Ref: NY176266

Date: ....

Ascent start time: .... Peak time: ....

Descent start time: .... Finish time: ....

Ascent duration: .... Descent duration: ....

Total time: [   ]

Total distance covered:...

Companions:...

....

Local Pub: .... ☆☆☆☆☆

Weather conditions:...

....

Difficulty: (poor) ○ ○ ○ ○ ○ ○ ○ ○ ○ (great)

Views: (poor) ○ ○ ○ ○ ○ ○ ○ ○ ○ (great)

Enjoyment: (poor) ○ ○ ○ ○ ○ ○ ○ ○ ○ (great)

Notes/pics:

Catbells

Region: North Western Fells
Height: 451m / 1,480ft
OS Grid Ref: NY244198

Date: ....

Ascent start time: .... Peak time: ....

Descent start time: .... Finish time: ....

Ascent duration: .... Descent duration: ....

Total time: [   ]

Total distance covered:..

Companions:..

....

Local Pub: .... ☆ ☆ ☆ ☆ ☆

Weather conditions:..

....

Difficulty: (poor) ○ ○ ○ ○ ○ ○ ○ ○ ○ (great)

Views: (poor) ○ ○ ○ ○ ○ ○ ○ ○ ○ (great)

Enjoyment: (poor) ○ ○ ○ ○ ○ ○ ○ ○ ○ (great)

Notes/pics:

Barrow

Region: North Western Fells
Height: 455m / 1,493ft
OS Grid Ref: NY227218

Date: ....

Ascent start time: .... Peak time: ....

Descent start time: .... Finish time: ....

Ascent duration: .... Descent duration: ....

Total time: ┌─────────────────┐
           └─────────────────┘

Total distance covered:...

Companions:...

....

Local Pub: .... ☆ ☆ ☆ ☆ ☆

Weather conditions:...

....

Difficulty: (poor) ○ ○ ○ ○ ○ ○ ○ ○ ○ (great)

Views: (poor) ○ ○ ○ ○ ○ ○ ○ ○ ○ (great)

Enjoyment: (poor) ○ ○ ○ ○ ○ ○ ○ ○ ○ (great)

Notes/pics:

Barf

Region: North Western Fells
Height: 469m / 1,539ft
OS Grid Ref: NY214267

Date: ....

Ascent start time: .... Peak time: ....

Descent start time: .... Finish time: ....

Ascent duration: .... Descent duration: ....

Total time: [   ]

Total distance covered:...

Companions:...

....

Local Pub: .... ☆ ☆ ☆ ☆ ☆

Weather conditions:..

....

Difficulty: (poor) ○ ○ ○ ○ ○ ○ ○ ○ ○ (great)

Views: (poor) ○ ○ ○ ○ ○ ○ ○ ○ ○ (great)

Enjoyment: (poor) ○ ○ ○ ○ ○ ○ ○ ○ ○ (great)

Notes/pics:

Broom Fell

Region: North Western Fells
Height: 511m / 1,677ft
OS Grid Ref: NY194271

Date: ....

Ascent start time: .... Peak time: ....

Descent start time: .... Finish time: ....

Ascent duration: .... Descent duration: ....

Total time: [   ]

Total distance covered:...

Companions:...

....

Local Pub: .... ☆ ☆ ☆ ☆ ☆

Weather conditions:..

....

Difficulty: (poor) ○ ○ ○ ○ ○ ○ ○ ○ ○ (great)

Views: (poor) ○ ○ ○ ○ ○ ○ ○ ○ ○ (great)

Enjoyment: (poor) ○ ○ ○ ○ ○ ○ ○ ○ ○ (great)

Notes/pics:

Whinlatter (Brown How)

Region: North Western Fells
Height: 517m / 1,696ft
OS Grid Ref: NY191251

Date: ....

Ascent start time: .... Peak time: ....

Descent start time: .... Finish time: ....

Ascent duration: .... Descent duration: ....

Total time: [   ]

Total distance covered:..

Companions:...

....

Local Pub: .... ☆ ☆ ☆ ☆ ☆

Weather conditions:..

....

Difficulty: (poor) ○ ○ ○ ○ ○ ○ ○ ○ ○ (great)

Views: (poor) ○ ○ ○ ○ ○ ○ ○ ○ ○ (great)

Enjoyment: (poor) ○ ○ ○ ○ ○ ○ ○ ○ ○ (great)

Notes/pics:

Knott Rigg

Region: North Western Fells
Height: 556m / 1,824ft
OS Grid Ref: NY197188

Date: ....

Ascent start time: .... Peak time: ....

Descent start time: .... Finish time: ....

Ascent duration: .... Descent duration: ....

Total time: [   ]

Total distance covered:...

Companions:...

....

Local Pub: .... ☆ ☆ ☆ ☆ ☆

Weather conditions:...

....

Difficulty: (poor) ○ ○ ○ ○ ○ ○ ○ ○ ○ (great)

Views: (poor) ○ ○ ○ ○ ○ ○ ○ ○ ○ (great)

Enjoyment: (poor) ○ ○ ○ ○ ○ ○ ○ ○ ○ (great)

Notes/pics:

Lord's Seat

Region: North Western Fells
Height: 552m / 1,811ft
OS Grid Ref: NY204265

Date: ....

Ascent start time: .... Peak time: ....

Descent start time: .... Finish time: ....

Ascent duration: .... Descent duration: ....

Total time: [   ]

Total distance covered:...

Companions:...

....

Local Pub: .... ☆☆☆☆☆

Weather conditions:...

....

Difficulty: (poor) ○ ○ ○ ○ ○ ○ ○ ○ ○ ○ (great)

Views: (poor) ○ ○ ○ ○ ○ ○ ○ ○ ○ ○ (great)

Enjoyment: (poor) ○ ○ ○ ○ ○ ○ ○ ○ ○ ○ (great)

Notes/pics:

Ard Crags

Region: North Western Fells
Height: 581m / 1,906ft
OS Grid Ref: NY206197

Date: ....

Ascent start time: .... Peak time: ....

Descent start time: .... Finish time: ....

Ascent duration: .... Descent duration: ....

Total time: [   ]

Total distance covered:...

Companions:..

....

Local Pub: .... ☆☆☆☆☆

Weather conditions:...

....

Difficulty: (poor) O O O O O O O O O O (great)

Views: (poor) O O O O O O O O O O (great)

Enjoyment: (poor) O O O O O O O O O O (great)

Notes/pics:

Outerside

Region: North Western Fells
Height: 568m / 1,864ft
OS Grid Ref: NY211214

Date: ....

Ascent start time: .... Peak time: ....

Descent start time: .... Finish time: ....

Ascent duration: .... Descent duration: ....

Total time: [   ]

Total distance covered:...

Companions:...
....

Local Pub: .... ☆ ☆ ☆ ☆ ☆

Weather conditions:...
....

Difficulty: (poor) ○ ○ ○ ○ ○ ○ ○ ○ ○ (great)

Views: (poor) ○ ○ ○ ○ ○ ○ ○ ○ ○ (great)

Enjoyment: (poor) ○ ○ ○ ○ ○ ○ ○ ○ ○ (great)

Notes/pics:

Maiden Moor

Region: North Western Fells
Height: 575m / 1,886ft
OS Grid Ref: NY236181

Date: ....

Ascent start time: .... Peak time: ....

Descent start time: .... Finish time: ....

Ascent duration: .... Descent duration: ....

Total time: [   ]

Total distance covered:...

Companions:..

....

Local Pub: .... ☆☆☆☆☆

Weather conditions:..

....

Difficulty: (poor) ○ ○ ○ ○ ○ ○ ○ ○ ○ (great)

Views: (poor) ○ ○ ○ ○ ○ ○ ○ ○ ○ (great)

Enjoyment: (poor) ○ ○ ○ ○ ○ ○ ○ ○ ○ (great)

Notes/pics:

Causey Pike

Region: North Western Fells
Height: 637m / 2,090ft
OS Grid Ref: NY218208

Date: ....

Ascent start time: .... Peak time: ....

Descent start time: .... Finish time: ....

Ascent duration: .... Descent duration: ....

Total time: [   ]

Total distance covered:...

Companions:...

....

Local Pub: .... ☆ ☆ ☆ ☆ ☆

Weather conditions:...

....

Difficulty: (poor) ○ ○ ○ ○ ○ ○ ○ ○ ○ (great)

Views: (poor) ○ ○ ○ ○ ○ ○ ○ ○ ○ (great)

Enjoyment: (poor) ○ ○ ○ ○ ○ ○ ○ ○ ○ (great)

Notes/pics:

High Spy

Region: North Western Fells
Height: 653m / 2,143ft
OS Grid Ref: NY234162

Date: ....

Ascent start time: .... Peak time: ....

Descent start time: .... Finish time: ....

Ascent duration: .... Descent duration: ....

Total time: [   ]

Total distance covered:..

Companions:..

....

Local Pub: .... ☆☆☆☆☆

Weather conditions:..

....

Difficulty: (poor) ○ ○ ○ ○ ○ ○ ○ ○ ○ (great)

Views: (poor) ○ ○ ○ ○ ○ ○ ○ ○ ○ (great)

Enjoyment: (poor) ○ ○ ○ ○ ○ ○ ○ ○ ○ (great)

Notes/pics:

Whiteless Pike

Region: North Western Fells
Height: 660m / 2,165ft
OS Grid Ref: NY180189

Date: ....

Ascent start time: .... Peak time: ....

Descent start time: .... Finish time: ....

Ascent duration: .... Descent duration: ....

Total time: [   ]

Total distance covered:...

Companions:..

....

Local Pub: .... ☆ ☆ ☆ ☆ ☆

Weather conditions:..

....

Difficulty: (poor) ○ ○ ○ ○ ○ ○ ○ ○ ○ (great)

Views: (poor) ○ ○ ○ ○ ○ ○ ○ ○ ○ (great)

Enjoyment: (poor) ○ ○ ○ ○ ○ ○ ○ ○ ○ (great)

Notes/pics:

Scar Crags

Region: North Western Fells
Height: 672m / 2,205ft
OS Grid Ref: NY208206

Date: ....

Ascent start time: .... Peak time: ....

Descent start time: .... Finish time: ....

Ascent duration: .... Descent duration: ....

Total time:

Total distance covered:...

Companions:...

....

Local Pub: .... ☆ ☆ ☆ ☆ ☆

Weather conditions:...

....

Difficulty: (poor) O O O O O O O O O O (great)

Views: (poor) O O O O O O O O O O (great)

Enjoyment: (poor) O O O O O O O O O O (great)

Notes/pics:

Whiteside (West Top)

Region: North Western Fells
Height: 707m / 2,320ft
OS Grid Ref: NY170219

Date: ....

Ascent start time: .... Peak time: ....

Descent start time: .... Finish time: ....

Ascent duration: .... Descent duration: ....

Total time: [   ]

Total distance covered: ....

Companions: ....

....

Local Pub: .... ☆☆☆☆☆

Weather conditions: ....

....

Difficulty: (poor) ○ ○ ○ ○ ○ ○ ○ ○ ○ (great)

Views: (poor) ○ ○ ○ ○ ○ ○ ○ ○ ○ (great)

Enjoyment: (poor) ○ ○ ○ ○ ○ ○ ○ ○ ○ (great)

Notes/pics:

Hindscarth

Region: North Western Fells
Height: 727m / 2,385ft
OS Grid Ref: NY215165

Date: ....

Ascent start time: .... Peak time: ....

Descent start time: .... Finish time: ....

Ascent duration: .... Descent duration: ....

Total time: [   ]

Total distance covered:...

Companions:..

....

Local Pub: .... ☆ ☆ ☆ ☆ ☆

Weather conditions:...

....

Difficulty: (poor) ○ ○ ○ ○ ○ ○ ○ ○ ○ (great)

Views: (poor) ○ ○ ○ ○ ○ ○ ○ ○ ○ (great)

Enjoyment: (poor) ○ ○ ○ ○ ○ ○ ○ ○ ○ (great)

Notes/pics:

Robinson

Region: North Western Fells
Height: 737m / 2,418ft
OS Grid Ref: NY201168

Date: ....

Ascent start time: .... Peak time: ....

Descent start time: .... Finish time: ....

Ascent duration: .... Descent duration: ....

Total time: [   ]

Total distance covered:...

Companions:...

....

Local Pub: .... ☆ ☆ ☆ ☆ ☆

Weather conditions:..

....

Difficulty: (poor) ○ ○ ○ ○ ○ ○ ○ ○ ○ ○ (great)

Views: (poor) ○ ○ ○ ○ ○ ○ ○ ○ ○ ○ (great)

Enjoyment: (poor) ○ ○ ○ ○ ○ ○ ○ ○ ○ ○ (great)

Notes/pics:

Dale Head

Region: North Western Fells
Height: 753m / 2,470ft
OS Grid Ref: NY222153

Date: ....

Ascent start time: .... Peak time: ....

Descent start time: .... Finish time: ....

Ascent duration: .... Descent duration: ....

Total time: [   ]

Total distance covered:...

Companions:..

....

Local Pub: .... ☆ ☆ ☆ ☆ ☆

Weather conditions:..

....

Difficulty: (poor) ○ ○ ○ ○ ○ ○ ○ ○ ○ ○ (great)

Views: (poor) ○ ○ ○ ○ ○ ○ ○ ○ ○ ○ (great)

Enjoyment: (poor) ○ ○ ○ ○ ○ ○ ○ ○ ○ ○ (great)

Notes/pics:

Hopegill Head

Region: North Western Fells
Height: 770m / 2,526ft
OS Grid Ref: NY185221

Date: ....

Ascent start time: .... Peak time: ....

Descent start time: .... Finish time: ....

Ascent duration: .... Descent duration: ....

Total time: [   ]

Total distance covered:...

Companions:..

....

Local Pub: .... ☆ ☆ ☆ ☆ ☆

Weather conditions:..

....

Difficulty: (poor) ○ ○ ○ ○ ○ ○ ○ ○ ○ (great)

Views: (poor) ○ ○ ○ ○ ○ ○ ○ ○ ○ (great)

Enjoyment: (poor) ○ ○ ○ ○ ○ ○ ○ ○ ○ (great)

Notes/pics:

Sail

Region: North Western Fells
Height: 773m / 2,536ft
OS Grid Ref: NY198202

Date: ....

Ascent start time: .... Peak time: ....

Descent start time: .... Finish time: ....

Ascent duration: .... Descent duration: ....

Total time: [   ]

Total distance covered:...

Companions:..

....

Local Pub: .... ☆ ☆ ☆ ☆ ☆

Weather conditions:..

....

Difficulty: (poor) O O O O O O O O O (great)

Views: (poor) O O O O O O O O O (great)

Enjoyment: (poor) O O O O O O O O O (great)

Notes/pics:

Wandope

Region: North Western Fells
Height: 772m / 2,533ft
OS Grid Ref: NY188197

Date: ....

Ascent start time: .... Peak time: ....

Descent start time: .... Finish time: ....

Ascent duration: .... Descent duration: ....

Total time: [   ]

Total distance covered:...

Companions:...

....

Local Pub: .... ☆ ☆ ☆ ☆ ☆

Weather conditions:...

....

Difficulty: (poor) ○ ○ ○ ○ ○ ○ ○ ○ ○ ○ (great)

Views: (poor) ○ ○ ○ ○ ○ ○ ○ ○ ○ ○ (great)

Enjoyment: (poor) ○ ○ ○ ○ ○ ○ ○ ○ ○ ○ (great)

Notes/pics:

Grisedale Pike

Region: North Western Fells
Height: 791m / 2,595ft
OS Grid Ref: NY198225

Date: ....

Ascent start time: .... Peak time: ....

Descent start time: .... Finish time: ....

Ascent duration: .... Descent duration: ....

Total time: [   ]

Total distance covered:...

Companions:..

....

Local Pub: .... ☆ ☆ ☆ ☆ ☆

Weather conditions:...

....

Difficulty: (poor) ○ ○ ○ ○ ○ ○ ○ ○ ○ ○ (great)

Views: (poor) ○ ○ ○ ○ ○ ○ ○ ○ ○ ○ (great)

Enjoyment: (poor) ○ ○ ○ ○ ○ ○ ○ ○ ○ ○ (great)

Notes/pics:

Crag Hill (Eel Crag)

Region: North Western Fells
Height: 839m / 2,753ft
OS Grid Ref: NY192203

Date: ....

Ascent start time: .... Peak time: ....

Descent start time: .... Finish time: ....

Ascent duration: .... Descent duration: ....

Total time: [   ]

Total distance covered:...

Companions:..

....

Local Pub: .... ☆ ☆ ☆ ☆ ☆

Weather conditions:...

....

Difficulty: (poor) ○ ○ ○ ○ ○ ○ ○ ○ ○ (great)

Views: (poor) ○ ○ ○ ○ ○ ○ ○ ○ ○ (great)

Enjoyment: (poor) ○ ○ ○ ○ ○ ○ ○ ○ ○ (great)

Notes/pics:

Grasmoor

Region: North Western Fells
Height: 852m / 2,795ft
OS Grid Ref: NY174203

Date: ....

Ascent start time: .... Peak time: ....

Descent start time: .... Finish time: ....

Ascent duration: .... Descent duration: ....

Total time: [   ]

Total distance covered:...

Companions:..

....

Local Pub: .... ☆☆☆☆☆

Weather conditions:..

....

Difficulty: (poor) ○ ○ ○ ○ ○ ○ ○ ○ ○ (great)

Views: (poor) ○ ○ ○ ○ ○ ○ ○ ○ ○ (great)

Enjoyment: (poor) ○ ○ ○ ○ ○ ○ ○ ○ ○ (great)

Notes/pics:

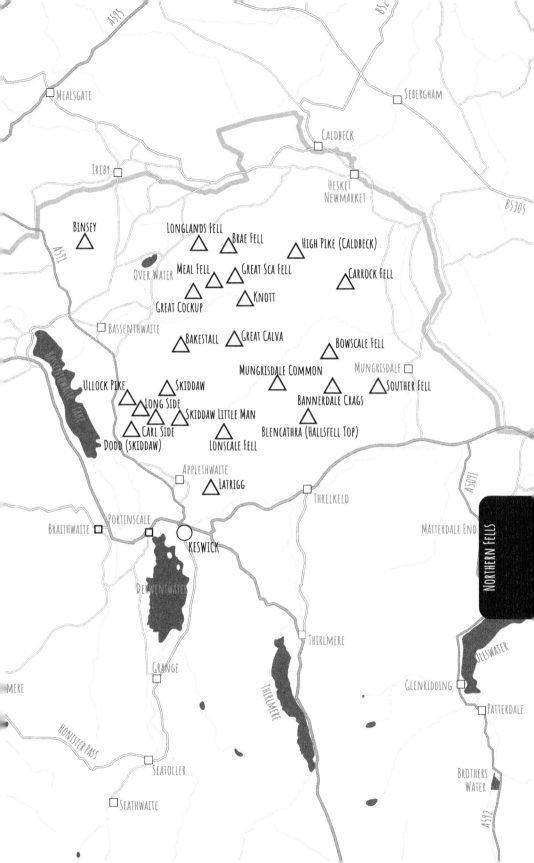

MEALSGATE

SEBERGHAM

CALDBECK

IREBY

HESKET
NEWMARKET

BS305

A591

BINSEY

LONGLANDS FELL

BRAE FELL

HIGH PIKE (CALDBECK)

OVER WATER

MEAL FELL

GREAT SCA FELL

CARROCK FELL

GREAT COCKUP

KNOTT

BASSENTHWAITE

BAKESTALL

GREAT CALVA

BOWSCALE FELL

MUNGRISDALE COMMON

MUNGRISDALE

ULLOCK PIKE

SKIDDAW

SOUTHER FELL

LONG SIDE

BANNERDALE CRAGS

SKIDDAW LITTLE MAN

CARL SIDE

BLENCATHRA (HALLSFELL TOP)

DODD (SKIDDAW)

LONSCALE FELL

APPLETHWAITE

LATRIGG

THRELKELD

PORTINSCALE

MATTERDALE END

BRAITHWAITE

KESWICK

A5091

DERWENTWATER

ULLSWATER

GRANGE

THIRLMERE

GLENRIDDING

MERE

PATTERDALE

THIRLMERE

HONISTER PASS

SEATOLLER

BROTHERS
WATER

SEATHWAITE

A592

Latrigg

Region: Northern Fells
Height: 368m / 1,207ft
OS Grid Ref: NY279247

Date: ....

Ascent start time: .... Peak time: ....

Descent start time: .... Finish time: ....

Ascent duration: .... Descent duration: ....

Total time: [   ]

Total distance covered:...

Companions:...

....

Local Pub: .... ☆☆☆☆☆

Weather conditions:...

....

Difficulty: (poor) ○ ○ ○ ○ ○ ○ ○ ○ ○ (great)

Views: (poor) ○ ○ ○ ○ ○ ○ ○ ○ ○ (great)

Enjoyment: (poor) ○ ○ ○ ○ ○ ○ ○ ○ ○ (great)

Notes/pics:

Binsey

Region: Northern Fells
Height: 447m / 1,467ft
OS Grid Ref: NY225355

Date: ....

Ascent start time: .... Peak time: ....

Descent start time: .... Finish time: ....

Ascent duration: .... Descent duration: ....

Total time: [ ]

Total distance covered:...

Companions:...

....

Local Pub: .... ☆ ☆ ☆ ☆ ☆

Weather conditions:..

....

Difficulty: (poor) ○ ○ ○ ○ ○ ○ ○ ○ ○ (great)

Views: (poor) ○ ○ ○ ○ ○ ○ ○ ○ ○ (great)

Enjoyment: (poor) ○ ○ ○ ○ ○ ○ ○ ○ ○ (great)

Notes/pics:

Longlands Fell

Region: Northern Fells
Height: 483m / 1,585ft
OS Grid Ref: NY275354

Date: ....

Ascent start time: .... Peak time: ....

Descent start time: .... Finish time: ....

Ascent duration: .... Descent duration: ....

Total time: [   ]

Total distance covered:...

Companions:..

....

Local Pub: .... ☆ ☆ ☆ ☆ ☆

Weather conditions:...

....

Difficulty: (poor) O O O O O O O O O O (great)

Views: (poor) O O O O O O O O O O (great)

Enjoyment: (poor) O O O O O O O O O O (great)

Notes/pics:

Dodd (Skiddaw)

Region: Northern Fells
Height: 502m / 1,647ft
OS Grid Ref: NY244273

Date: ....

Ascent start time: .... Peak time: ....

Descent start time: .... Finish time: ....

Ascent duration: .... Descent duration: ....

Total time: [   ]

Total distance covered:...

Companions:..

....

Local Pub: .... ☆ ☆ ☆ ☆ ☆

Weather conditions:...

....

Difficulty: (poor) ○ ○ ○ ○ ○ ○ ○ ○ ○ (great)

Views: (poor) ○ ○ ○ ○ ○ ○ ○ ○ ○ (great)

Enjoyment: (poor) ○ ○ ○ ○ ○ ○ ○ ○ ○ (great)

Notes/pics:

Souther Fell

Region: Northern Fells
Height: 522m / 1,713ft
OS Grid Ref: NY354291

Date: ....

Ascent start time: .... Peak time: ....

Descent start time: .... Finish time: ....

Ascent duration: .... Descent duration: ....

Total time: [   ]

Total distance covered: ....

Companions: ....

....

Local Pub: .... ☆ ☆ ☆ ☆ ☆

Weather conditions: ....

....

Difficulty: (poor) ○ ○ ○ ○ ○ ○ ○ ○ ○ (great)

Views: (poor) ○ ○ ○ ○ ○ ○ ○ ○ ○ (great)

Enjoyment: (poor) ○ ○ ○ ○ ○ ○ ○ ○ ○ (great)

Notes/pics:

Great Cockup

Region: Northern Fells
Height: 526m / 1,726ft
OS Grid Ref: NY273333

Date: ....

Ascent start time: .... Peak time: ....

Descent start time: .... Finish time: ....

Ascent duration: .... Descent duration: ....

Total time: [   ]

Total distance covered:..

Companions:..

....

Local Pub: .... ☆ ☆ ☆ ☆ ☆

Weather conditions:..

....

Difficulty: (poor) ○ ○ ○ ○ ○ ○ ○ ○ ○ (great)

Views: (poor) ○ ○ ○ ○ ○ ○ ○ ○ ○ (great)

Enjoyment: (poor) ○ ○ ○ ○ ○ ○ ○ ○ ○ (great)

Notes/pics:

139

Meal Fell

Region: Northern Fells
Height: 550m / 1,804ft
OS Grid Ref: NY283337

Date: ....

Ascent start time: .... Peak time: ....

Descent start time: .... Finish time: ....

Ascent duration: .... Descent duration: ....

Total time: [   ]

Total distance covered:...

Companions:..

....

Local Pub: .... ☆☆☆☆☆

Weather conditions:..

....

Difficulty: (poor) ○ ○ ○ ○ ○ ○ ○ ○ ○ (great)

Views: (poor) ○ ○ ○ ○ ○ ○ ○ ○ ○ (great)

Enjoyment: (poor) ○ ○ ○ ○ ○ ○ ○ ○ ○ (great)

Notes/pics:

Brae Fell

Region: Northern Fells
Height: 586m / 1,923ft
OS Grid Ref: NY288351

Date: ....

Ascent start time: .... Peak time: ....

Descent start time: .... Finish time: ....

Ascent duration: .... Descent duration: ....

Total time: [   ]

Total distance covered:..

Companions:...

....

Local Pub: .... ☆ ☆ ☆ ☆ ☆

Weather conditions:...

....

Difficulty: (poor) ○ ○ ○ ○ ○ ○ ○ ○ ○ ○ (great)

Views: (poor) ○ ○ ○ ○ ○ ○ ○ ○ ○ ○ (great)

Enjoyment: (poor) ○ ○ ○ ○ ○ ○ ○ ○ ○ ○ (great)

Notes/pics:

Mungrisdale Common

Region: Northern Fells
Height: 633m / 2,077ft
OS Grid Ref: NY310292

Date: ....

Ascent start time: .... Peak time: ....

Descent start time: .... Finish time: ....

Ascent duration: .... Descent duration: ....

Total time:

Total distance covered:...

Companions:...

....

Local Pub: .... ☆☆☆☆☆

Weather conditions:..

....

Difficulty: (poor) ○ ○ ○ ○ ○ ○ ○ ○ ○ ○ (great)

Views: (poor) ○ ○ ○ ○ ○ ○ ○ ○ ○ ○ (great)

Enjoyment: (poor) ○ ○ ○ ○ ○ ○ ○ ○ ○ ○ (great)

Notes/pics:

Great Sca Fell

Region: Northern Fells
Height: 651m / 2,136ft
OS Grid Ref: NY291339

Date: ....

Ascent start time: .... Peak time: ....

Descent start time: .... Finish time: ....

Ascent duration: .... Descent duration: ....

Total time: [   ]

Total distance covered: ....

Companions: ....

....

Local Pub: .... ☆ ☆ ☆ ☆ ☆

Weather conditions: ....

....

Difficulty: (poor) ○ ○ ○ ○ ○ ○ ○ ○ ○ ○ (great)

Views: (poor) ○ ○ ○ ○ ○ ○ ○ ○ ○ ○ (great)

Enjoyment: (poor) ○ ○ ○ ○ ○ ○ ○ ○ ○ ○ (great)

Notes/pics:

High Pike (Caldbeck)

Region: Northern Fells
Height: 658m / 2,159ft
OS Grid Ref: NY318350

Date: ....

Ascent start time: .... Peak time: ....

Descent start time: .... Finish time: ....

Ascent duration: .... Descent duration: ....

Total time: [   ]

Total distance covered:...

Companions:..

....

Local Pub: .... ☆ ☆ ☆ ☆ ☆

Weather conditions:..

....

Difficulty: (poor) ○ ○ ○ ○ ○ ○ ○ ○ ○ ○ (great)

Views: (poor) ○ ○ ○ ○ ○ ○ ○ ○ ○ ○ (great)

Enjoyment: (poor) ○ ○ ○ ○ ○ ○ ○ ○ ○ ○ (great)

Notes/pics:

Carrock Fell

Region: Northern Fells
Height: 663m / 2,175ft
OS Grid Ref: NY341336

Date: ....

Ascent start time: .... Peak time: ....

Descent start time: .... Finish time: ....

Ascent duration: .... Descent duration: ....

Total time: [   ]

Total distance covered:...

Companions:..

....

Local Pub: .... ☆ ☆ ☆ ☆ ☆

Weather conditions:...

....

Difficulty: (poor) ○ ○ ○ ○ ○ ○ ○ ○ ○ (great)

Views: (poor) ○ ○ ○ ○ ○ ○ ○ ○ ○ (great)

Enjoyment: (poor) ○ ○ ○ ○ ○ ○ ○ ○ ○ (great)

Notes/pics:

Bakestall

Region: Northern Fells
Height: 673m / 2,208ft
OS Grid Ref: NY266308

Date: ....

Ascent start time: .... Peak time: ....

Descent start time: .... Finish time: ....

Ascent duration: .... Descent duration: ....

Total time: [   ]

Total distance covered:...

Companions:...

....

Local Pub: .... ☆ ☆ ☆ ☆ ☆

Weather conditions:...

....

Difficulty: (poor) ○ ○ ○ ○ ○ ○ ○ ○ ○ ○ (great)

Views: (poor) ○ ○ ○ ○ ○ ○ ○ ○ ○ ○ (great)

Enjoyment: (poor) ○ ○ ○ ○ ○ ○ ○ ○ ○ ○ (great)

Notes/pics:

Bannerdale Crags

Region: Northern Fells
Height: 683m / 2,241ft
OS Grid Ref: NY335290

Date: ....

Ascent start time: .... Peak time: ....

Descent start time: .... Finish time: ....

Ascent duration: .... Descent duration: ....

Total time: [   ]

Total distance covered:..

Companions:..

....

Local Pub: .... ☆ ☆ ☆ ☆ ☆

Weather conditions:..

....

Difficulty: (poor) ○ ○ ○ ○ ○ ○ ○ ○ ○ ○ (great)

Views: (poor) ○ ○ ○ ○ ○ ○ ○ ○ ○ ○ (great)

Enjoyment: (poor) ○ ○ ○ ○ ○ ○ ○ ○ ○ ○ (great)

Notes/pics:

Ullock Pike

Region: Northern Fells
Height: 690m / 2,264ft
OS Grid Ref: NY244287

Date: ....

Ascent start time: .... Peak time: ....

Descent start time: .... Finish time: ....

Ascent duration: .... Descent duration: ....

Total time: [   ]

Total distance covered:...

Companions:..

....

Local Pub: .... ☆☆☆☆☆

Weather conditions:..

....

Difficulty: (poor) ○ ○ ○ ○ ○ ○ ○ ○ ○ (great)

Views: (poor) ○ ○ ○ ○ ○ ○ ○ ○ ○ (great)

Enjoyment: (poor) ○ ○ ○ ○ ○ ○ ○ ○ ○ (great)

Notes/pics:

Great Calva

Region: Northern Fells
Height: 690m / 2,264ft
OS Grid Ref: NY290311

Date: ....

Ascent start time: .... Peak time: ....

Descent start time: .... Finish time: ....

Ascent duration: .... Descent duration: ....

Total time: [   ]

Total distance covered:...

Companions:..

....

Local Pub: .... ☆☆☆☆☆

Weather conditions:...

....

Difficulty: (poor) ○ ○ ○ ○ ○ ○ ○ ○ ○ (great)

Views: (poor) ○ ○ ○ ○ ○ ○ ○ ○ ○ (great)

Enjoyment: (poor) ○ ○ ○ ○ ○ ○ ○ ○ ○ (great)

Notes/pics:

Bowscale Fell

Region: Northern Fells
Height: 702m / 2,303ft
OS Grid Ref: NY333305

Date: ....

Ascent start time: .... Peak time: ....

Descent start time: .... Finish time: ....

Ascent duration: .... Descent duration: ....

Total time: [   ]

Total distance covered:..

Companions:..

....

Local Pub: .... ☆ ☆ ☆ ☆ ☆

Weather conditions:..

....

Difficulty: (poor) O O O O O O O O O O (great)

Views: (poor) O O O O O O O O O O (great)

Enjoyment: (poor) O O O O O O O O O O (great)

Notes/pics:

150

Knott

Region: Northern Fells
Height: 710m / 2,329ft
OS Grid Ref: NY296329

Date: ....

Ascent start time: .... Peak time: ....

Descent start time: .... Finish time: ....

Ascent duration: .... Descent duration: ....

Total time: [   ]

Total distance covered:..

Companions:..

....

Local Pub: .... ☆ ☆ ☆ ☆ ☆

Weather conditions:..

....

Difficulty: (poor) ○ ○ ○ ○ ○ ○ ○ ○ ○ (great)

Views: (poor) ○ ○ ○ ○ ○ ○ ○ ○ ○ (great)

Enjoyment: (poor) ○ ○ ○ ○ ○ ○ ○ ○ ○ (great)

Notes/pics:

Lonscale Fell

Region: Northern Fells
Height: 715m / 2,346ft
OS Grid Ref: NY285271

Date: ....

Ascent start time: .... Peak time: ....

Descent start time: .... Finish time: ....

Ascent duration: .... Descent duration: ....

Total time: [   ]

Total distance covered:...

Companions:...

....

Local Pub: .... ☆☆☆☆☆

Weather conditions:...

....

Difficulty: (poor) ○ ○ ○ ○ ○ ○ ○ ○ ○ (great)

Views: (poor) ○ ○ ○ ○ ○ ○ ○ ○ ○ (great)

Enjoyment: (poor) ○ ○ ○ ○ ○ ○ ○ ○ ○ (great)

Notes/pics:

Long Side

Region: Northern Fells
Height: 734m / 2,408ft
OS Grid Ref: NY248284

Date: ....

Ascent start time: .... Peak time: ....

Descent start time: .... Finish time: ....

Ascent duration: .... Descent duration: ....

Total time: [   ]

Total distance covered:...

Companions:...

....

Local Pub: .... ☆☆☆☆☆

Weather conditions:...

....

Difficulty: (poor) ○ ○ ○ ○ ○ ○ ○ ○ ○ (great)

Views: (poor) ○ ○ ○ ○ ○ ○ ○ ○ ○ (great)

Enjoyment: (poor) ○ ○ ○ ○ ○ ○ ○ ○ ○ (great)

Notes/pics:

Carl Side

Region: Northern Fells
Height: 746m / 2,448ft
OS Grid Ref: NY254280

Date: ....

Ascent start time: .... Peak time: ....

Descent start time: .... Finish time: ....

Ascent duration: .... Descent duration: ....

Total time: [   ]

Total distance covered:...

Companions:...

....

Local Pub: .... ☆☆☆☆☆

Weather conditions:..

....

Difficulty: (poor) ○ ○ ○ ○ ○ ○ ○ ○ ○ (great)

Views: (poor) ○ ○ ○ ○ ○ ○ ○ ○ ○ (great)

Enjoyment: (poor) ○ ○ ○ ○ ○ ○ ○ ○ ○ (great)

Notes/pics:

Skiddaw Little Man

Region: Northern Fells
Height: 865m / 2,838ft
OS Grid Ref: NY266277

Date: ....

Ascent start time: ....   Peak time: ....

Descent start time: ....   Finish time: ....

Ascent duration: ....   Descent duration: ....

Total time: [   ]

Total distance covered:...

Companions:...

....

Local Pub: .... ☆ ☆ ☆ ☆ ☆

Weather conditions:..

....

Difficulty: (poor) ○ ○ ○ ○ ○ ○ ○ ○ ○ (great)

Views: (poor) ○ ○ ○ ○ ○ ○ ○ ○ ○ (great)

Enjoyment: (poor) ○ ○ ○ ○ ○ ○ ○ ○ ○ (great)

Notes/pics:

Blencathra (Hallsfell Top)

Region: Northern Fells
Height: 868m / 2,848ft
OS Grid Ref: NY323277

Date: ....

Ascent start time: .... Peak time: ....

Descent start time: .... Finish time: ....

Ascent duration: .... Descent duration: ....

Total time: [   ]

Total distance covered:..

Companions:..

....

Local Pub: .... ☆☆☆☆☆

Weather conditions:...

....

Difficulty: (poor) ○ ○ ○ ○ ○ ○ ○ ○ ○ ○ (great)

Views: (poor) ○ ○ ○ ○ ○ ○ ○ ○ ○ ○ (great)

Enjoyment: (poor) ○ ○ ○ ○ ○ ○ ○ ○ ○ ○ (great)

Notes/pics:

Skiddaw

Region: Northern Fells
Height: 931m / 3,054ft
OS Grid Ref: NY260290

Date: ....

Ascent start time: .... Peak time: ....

Descent start time: .... Finish time: ....

Ascent duration: .... Descent duration: ....

Total time: [   ]

Total distance covered:...

Companions:...

....

Local Pub: .... ☆☆☆☆☆

Weather conditions:...

....

Difficulty: (poor) ○ ○ ○ ○ ○ ○ ○ ○ ○ (great)

Views: (poor) ○ ○ ○ ○ ○ ○ ○ ○ ○ (great)

Enjoyment: (poor) ○ ○ ○ ○ ○ ○ ○ ○ ○ (great)

Notes/pics:

CRUMMOCK WATER

BUTTERMERE

BUTTERMERE

HONISTER PASS

GRANGE

THIRLMERE

THIRLMERE

GLENR

SEATOLLER

SEATHWAITE

△ Rosthwaite Fell

Seathwaite Fell △   △ Glaramara

GRASMERE   Grasmere

Grasmere ○

RYDALWATER   RYDA

WASDALE HEAD

Lingmell △   Great End △   △ Allen Crags

Scafell Pike △   Esk Pike △   △ Rosset Pike

CHAPEL STILE

WAST WATER

Scafell △   △ Bowfell

 Illgill Head △   Slight Side △

Crinkle Crags △

ELTERWATER   Elterwater

Pike of Blisco △   △

△ Cold Pike   Lingmoor Fell

ELTER WATER

SKELWITH BRIDGE

Whin Rigg (Wasdale) △

△ Hard Knott

HARDKNOTT PASS   WRYNOSE PASS

ESKDALE GREEN

BOOT

Grey Friar △   Great Carrs △△   Holme Fell △   △ Black Fell

A593

Harter Fell (Eskdale) △   Swirl How   Wetherlam

HAWKSHEAD

Green Crag △   Brim Fell △

Dow Crag △   △ Old Man of Coniston

Coniston ○

ESTHW

GRIZEDALE

TORVER

CONISTON WATER

SATTERTHWAITE

ULPHA

A5084

SOUTHERN FELLS

BLAWITH

BROUGHTON IN FURNESS ○

NEWBY BRIDGE

Holme Fell

Region: Southern Fells
Height: 317m / 1,040ft
OS Grid Ref: NY315006

Date: ....

Ascent start time: .... Peak time: ....

Descent start time: .... Finish time: ....

Ascent duration: .... Descent duration: ....

Total time: [   ]

Total distance covered:..

Companions:..

....

Local Pub: .... ☆ ☆ ☆ ☆ ☆

Weather conditions:..

....

Difficulty: (poor) ○ ○ ○ ○ ○ ○ ○ ○ ○ (great)

Views: (poor) ○ ○ ○ ○ ○ ○ ○ ○ ○ (great)

Enjoyment: (poor) ○ ○ ○ ○ ○ ○ ○ ○ ○ (great)

Notes/pics:

Black Fell

Region: Southern Fells
Height: 323m / 1,060ft
OS Grid Ref: NY340015

Date: ....

Ascent start time: .... Peak time: ....

Descent start time: .... Finish time: ....

Ascent duration: .... Descent duration: ....

Total time: [   ]

Total distance covered:...

Companions:...

....

Local Pub: .... ☆ ☆ ☆ ☆ ☆

Weather conditions:...

....

Difficulty: (poor) ○ ○ ○ ○ ○ ○ ○ ○ ○ (great)

Views: (poor) ○ ○ ○ ○ ○ ○ ○ ○ ○ (great)

Enjoyment: (poor) ○ ○ ○ ○ ○ ○ ○ ○ ○ (great)

Notes/pics:

Lingmoor Fell

Region: Southern Fells
Height: 470m / 1,542ft
OS Grid Ref: NY302046

Date: ....

Ascent start time: .... Peak time: ....

Descent start time: .... Finish time: ....

Ascent duration: .... Descent duration: ....

Total time: [ ]

Total distance covered:..

Companions:..

....

Local Pub: .... ☆☆☆☆☆

Weather conditions:..

....

Difficulty: (poor) ○ ○ ○ ○ ○ ○ ○ ○ ○ (great)

Views: (poor) ○ ○ ○ ○ ○ ○ ○ ○ ○ (great)

Enjoyment: (poor) ○ ○ ○ ○ ○ ○ ○ ○ ○ (great)

Notes/pics:

Green Crag

Region: Southern Fells
Height: 489m / 1,603ft
OS Grid Ref: SD200982

Date: ....

Ascent start time: .... Peak time: ....

Descent start time: .... Finish time: ....

Ascent duration: .... Descent duration: ....

Total time: [   ]

Total distance covered:...

Companions:...

....

Local Pub: .... ☆ ☆ ☆ ☆ ☆

Weather conditions:..

....

Difficulty: (poor) ○ ○ ○ ○ ○ ○ ○ ○ ○ ○ (great)

Views: (poor) ○ ○ ○ ○ ○ ○ ○ ○ ○ ○ (great)

Enjoyment: (poor) ○ ○ ○ ○ ○ ○ ○ ○ ○ ○ (great)

Notes/pics:

Whin Rigg

Region: Southern Fells
Height: 537m / 1,762ft
OS Grid Ref: NY151035

Date: ....

Ascent start time: .... Peak time: ....

Descent start time: .... Finish time: ....

Ascent duration: .... Descent duration: ....

Total time: [   ]

Total distance covered:...

Companions:..

....

Local Pub: .... ☆☆☆☆☆

Weather conditions:...

....

Difficulty: (poor) ○ ○ ○ ○ ○ ○ ○ ○ ○ (great)

Views: (poor) ○ ○ ○ ○ ○ ○ ○ ○ ○ (great)

Enjoyment: (poor) ○ ○ ○ ○ ○ ○ ○ ○ ○ (great)

Notes/pics:

Hard Knott

Region: Southern Fells
Height: 549m / 1,801ft
OS Grid Ref: NY231023

Date: ....

Ascent start time: .... Peak time: ....

Descent start time: .... Finish time: ....

Ascent duration: .... Descent duration: ....

Total time: [   ]

Total distance covered:..

Companions:..

....

Local Pub: .... ☆ ☆ ☆ ☆ ☆

Weather conditions:..

....

Difficulty: (poor) ○ ○ ○ ○ ○ ○ ○ ○ ○ ○ (great)

Views: (poor) ○ ○ ○ ○ ○ ○ ○ ○ ○ ○ (great)

Enjoyment: (poor) ○ ○ ○ ○ ○ ○ ○ ○ ○ ○ (great)

Notes/pics:

Rosthwaite Fell

Region: Southern Fells
Height: 551m / 1,808ft
OS Grid Ref: NY258124

Date: ....

Ascent start time: .... Peak time: ....

Descent start time: .... Finish time: ....

Ascent duration: .... Descent duration: ....

Total time: [   ]

Total distance covered:...

Companions:...

....

Local Pub: .... ☆☆☆☆☆

Weather conditions:..

....

Difficulty: (poor) ○ ○ ○ ○ ○ ○ ○ ○ ○ ○ (great)

Views: (poor) ○ ○ ○ ○ ○ ○ ○ ○ ○ ○ (great)

Enjoyment: (poor) ○ ○ ○ ○ ○ ○ ○ ○ ○ ○ (great)

Notes/pics:

Seathwaite Fell

Region: Southern Fells
Height: 601m / 1,972ft
OS Grid Ref: NY229101

Date: ....

Ascent start time: .... Peak time: ....

Descent start time: .... Finish time: ....

Ascent duration: .... Descent duration: ....

Total time: [   ]

Total distance covered:...

Companions:..

....

Local Pub: .... ☆ ☆ ☆ ☆ ☆

Weather conditions:...

....

Difficulty: (poor) ○ ○ ○ ○ ○ ○ ○ ○ ○ (great)

Views: (poor) ○ ○ ○ ○ ○ ○ ○ ○ ○ (great)

Enjoyment: (poor) ○ ○ ○ ○ ○ ○ ○ ○ ○ (great)

Notes/pics:

Illgill Head

Region: Southern Fells
Height: 609m / 1,998ft
OS Grid Ref: NY168049

Date: ....

Ascent start time: .... Peak time: ....

Descent start time: .... Finish time: ....

Ascent duration: .... Descent duration: ....

Total time: [   ]

Total distance covered: ....

Companions: ....

....

Local Pub: .... ☆ ☆ ☆ ☆ ☆

Weather conditions: ....

....

Difficulty: (poor) ○ ○ ○ ○ ○ ○ ○ ○ ○ ○ (great)

Views: (poor) ○ ○ ○ ○ ○ ○ ○ ○ ○ ○ (great)

Enjoyment: (poor) ○ ○ ○ ○ ○ ○ ○ ○ ○ ○ (great)

Notes/pics:

Rosset Pike

Region: Southern Fells
Height: 651m / 2,136ft
OS Grid Ref: NY249075

Date: ....

Ascent start time: .... Peak time: ....

Descent start time: .... Finish time: ....

Ascent duration: .... Descent duration: ....

Total time: [   ]

Total distance covered:...

Companions:..

....

Local Pub: .... ☆ ☆ ☆ ☆ ☆

Weather conditions:...

....

Difficulty: (poor) ○ ○ ○ ○ ○ ○ ○ ○ ○ (great)

Views: (poor) ○ ○ ○ ○ ○ ○ ○ ○ ○ (great)

Enjoyment: (poor) ○ ○ ○ ○ ○ ○ ○ ○ ○ (great)

Notes/pics:

Harter Fell (Eskdale)

Region: Southern Fells
Height: 654m / 2,146ft
OS Grid Ref: SD218997

Date: ....

Ascent start time: .... Peak time: ....

Descent start time: .... Finish time: ....

Ascent duration: .... Descent duration: ....

Total time: [   ]

Total distance covered:...

Companions:...

....

Local Pub: .... ☆☆☆☆☆

Weather conditions:...

....

Difficulty: (poor) ○ ○ ○ ○ ○ ○ ○ ○ ○ (great)

Views: (poor) ○ ○ ○ ○ ○ ○ ○ ○ ○ (great)

Enjoyment: (poor) ○ ○ ○ ○ ○ ○ ○ ○ ○ (great)

Notes/pics:

Cold Pike

Region: Southern Fells
Height: 701m / 2,300ft
OS Grid Ref: NY262036

Date: ....

Ascent start time: .... Peak time: ....

Descent start time: .... Finish time: ....

Ascent duration: .... Descent duration: ....

Total time: [ ]

Total distance covered:...

Companions:...

....

Local Pub: .... ☆☆☆☆☆

Weather conditions:...

....

Difficulty: (poor) ○ ○ ○ ○ ○ ○ ○ ○ ○ (great)

Views: (poor) ○ ○ ○ ○ ○ ○ ○ ○ ○ (great)

Enjoyment: (poor) ○ ○ ○ ○ ○ ○ ○ ○ ○ (great)

Notes/pics:

Pike of Blisco

Region: Southern Fells
Height: 705m / 2,313ft
OS Grid Ref: NY271042

Date: ....

Ascent start time: .... Peak time: ....

Descent start time: .... Finish time: ....

Ascent duration: .... Descent duration: ....

Total time: [   ]

Total distance covered:..

Companions:..

....

Local Pub: .... ☆☆☆☆☆

Weather conditions:..

....

Difficulty: (poor) ○ ○ ○ ○ ○ ○ ○ ○ ○ ○ (great)

Views: (poor) ○ ○ ○ ○ ○ ○ ○ ○ ○ ○ (great)

Enjoyment: (poor) ○ ○ ○ ○ ○ ○ ○ ○ ○ ○ (great)

Notes/pics:

Slight Side

Region: Southern Fells
Height: 762m / 2,500ft
OS Grid Ref: NY209050

Date: ....

Ascent start time: .... Peak time: ....

Descent start time: .... Finish time: ....

Ascent duration: .... Descent duration: ....

Total time: [   ]

Total distance covered:..

Companions:..

....

Local Pub: .... ☆ ☆ ☆ ☆ ☆

Weather conditions:...

....

Difficulty: (poor) ○ ○ ○ ○ ○ ○ ○ ○ ○ ○ (great)

Views: (poor) ○ ○ ○ ○ ○ ○ ○ ○ ○ ○ (great)

Enjoyment: (poor) ○ ○ ○ ○ ○ ○ ○ ○ ○ ○ (great)

Notes/pics:

Wetherlam

Region: Southern Fells
Height: 763m / 2,503ft
OS Grid Ref: NY288011

Date: ....

Ascent start time: .... Peak time: ....

Descent start time: .... Finish time: ....

Ascent duration: .... Descent duration: ....

Total time: [   ]

Total distance covered:...

Companions:..

....

Local Pub: .... ☆ ☆ ☆ ☆ ☆

Weather conditions:..

....

Difficulty: (poor) ○ ○ ○ ○ ○ ○ ○ ○ ○ (great)

Views: (poor) ○ ○ ○ ○ ○ ○ ○ ○ ○ (great)

Enjoyment: (poor) ○ ○ ○ ○ ○ ○ ○ ○ ○ (great)

Notes/pics:

Grey Friar

Region: Southern Fells
Height: 773m / 2,536ft
OS Grid Ref: NY260003

Date: ....

Ascent start time: .... Peak time: ....

Descent start time: .... Finish time: ....

Ascent duration: .... Descent duration: ....

Total time: [ ]

Total distance covered:..

Companions:...

....

Local Pub: .... ☆ ☆ ☆ ☆ ☆

Weather conditions:..

....

Difficulty: (poor) ○ ○ ○ ○ ○ ○ ○ ○ ○ (great)

Views: (poor) ○ ○ ○ ○ ○ ○ ○ ○ ○ (great)

Enjoyment: (poor) ○ ○ ○ ○ ○ ○ ○ ○ ○ (great)

Notes/pics:

Dow Crag

Region: Southern Fells
Height: 778m / 2,552ft
OS Grid Ref: SD262977

Date: ....

Ascent start time: .... Peak time: ....

Descent start time: .... Finish time: ....

Ascent duration: .... Descent duration: ....

Total time: [   ]

Total distance covered: ....

Companions: ....
....

Local Pub: .... ☆ ☆ ☆ ☆ ☆

Weather conditions: ....
....

Difficulty: (poor) ○ ○ ○ ○ ○ ○ ○ ○ ○ (great)

Views: (poor) ○ ○ ○ ○ ○ ○ ○ ○ ○ (great)

Enjoyment: (poor) ○ ○ ○ ○ ○ ○ ○ ○ ○ (great)

Notes/pics:

Glaramara

Region: Southern Fells
Height: 783m / 2,569ft
OS Grid Ref: NY245104

Date: ....

Ascent start time: .... Peak time: ....

Descent start time: .... Finish time: ....

Ascent duration: .... Descent duration: ....

Total time: [   ]

Total distance covered:...

Companions:..

....

Local Pub: .... ☆ ☆ ☆ ☆ ☆

Weather conditions:...

....

Difficulty: (poor) ○ ○ ○ ○ ○ ○ ○ ○ ○ ○ (great)

Views: (poor) ○ ○ ○ ○ ○ ○ ○ ○ ○ ○ (great)

Enjoyment: (poor) ○ ○ ○ ○ ○ ○ ○ ○ ○ ○ (great)

Notes/pics:

Allen Crags

Region: Southern Fells
Height: 785m / 2,575ft
OS Grid Ref: NY236085

Date: ....

Ascent start time: .... Peak time: ....

Descent start time: .... Finish time: ....

Ascent duration: .... Descent duration: ....

Total time: [   ]

Total distance covered: ....

Companions: ....

....

Local Pub: .... ☆☆☆☆☆

Weather conditions: ....

....

Difficulty: (poor) ○ ○ ○ ○ ○ ○ ○ ○ ○ (great)

Views: (poor) ○ ○ ○ ○ ○ ○ ○ ○ ○ (great)

Enjoyment: (poor) ○ ○ ○ ○ ○ ○ ○ ○ ○ (great)

Notes/pics:

Great Carrs

Region: Southern Fells
Height: 785m / 2,575ft
OS Grid Ref: NY270009

Date: ....

Ascent start time: .... Peak time: ....

Descent start time: .... Finish time: ....

Ascent duration: .... Descent duration: ....

Total time: [   ]

Total distance covered:..

Companions:..

....

Local Pub: .... ☆ ☆ ☆ ☆ ☆

Weather conditions:..

....

Difficulty: (poor) ○ ○ ○ ○ ○ ○ ○ ○ ○ (great)

Views: (poor) ○ ○ ○ ○ ○ ○ ○ ○ ○ (great)

Enjoyment: (poor) ○ ○ ○ ○ ○ ○ ○ ○ ○ (great)

Notes/pics:

Brim Fell

Region: Southern Fells
Height: 796m / 2,612ft
OS Grid Ref: SD270985

Date: ....

Ascent start time: .... Peak time: ....

Descent start time: .... Finish time: ....

Ascent duration: .... Descent duration: ....

Total time: [   ]

Total distance covered: ....

Companions: ....

....

Local Pub: .... ☆☆☆☆☆

Weather conditions: ....

....

Difficulty: (poor) ○ ○ ○ ○ ○ ○ ○ ○ ○ ○ (great)

Views: (poor) ○ ○ ○ ○ ○ ○ ○ ○ ○ ○ (great)

Enjoyment: (poor) ○ ○ ○ ○ ○ ○ ○ ○ ○ ○ (great)

Notes/pics:

Swirl How

Region: Southern Fells
Height: 802m / 2,633ft
OS Grid Ref: NY272005

Date: ....

Ascent start time: .... Peak time: ....

Descent start time: .... Finish time: ....

Ascent duration: .... Descent duration: ....

Total time: [   ]

Total distance covered: ....

Companions: ....

....

Local Pub: .... ☆☆☆☆☆

Weather conditions: ....

....

Difficulty: (poor) ○ ○ ○ ○ ○ ○ ○ ○ ○ (great)

Views: (poor) ○ ○ ○ ○ ○ ○ ○ ○ ○ (great)

Enjoyment: (poor) ○ ○ ○ ○ ○ ○ ○ ○ ○ (great)

Notes/pics:

Old Man of Coniston

Region: Southern Fells
Height: 802m / 2,633ft
OS Grid Ref: SD272978

Date: ....

Ascent start time: .... Peak time: ....

Descent start time: .... Finish time: ....

Ascent duration: .... Descent duration: ....

Total time: [   ]

Total distance covered:...

Companions:...

....

Local Pub: .... ☆ ☆ ☆ ☆ ☆

Weather conditions:..

....

Difficulty: (poor) ○ ○ ○ ○ ○ ○ ○ ○ ○ (great)

Views: (poor) ○ ○ ○ ○ ○ ○ ○ ○ ○ (great)

Enjoyment: (poor) ○ ○ ○ ○ ○ ○ ○ ○ ○ (great)

Notes/pics:

Lingmell

Region: Southern Fells
Height: 807m / 2,648ft
OS Grid Ref: NY209081

Date: ....

Ascent start time: .... Peak time: ....

Descent start time: .... Finish time: ....

Ascent duration: .... Descent duration: ....

Total time: [   ]

Total distance covered: ....

Companions: ....

....

Local Pub: .... ☆ ☆ ☆ ☆ ☆

Weather conditions: ....

....

Difficulty: (poor) ○ ○ ○ ○ ○ ○ ○ ○ ○ ○ (great)

Views: (poor) ○ ○ ○ ○ ○ ○ ○ ○ ○ ○ (great)

Enjoyment: (poor) ○ ○ ○ ○ ○ ○ ○ ○ ○ ○ (great)

Notes/pics:

Crinkle Crags (Long Top)
Region: Southern Fells
Height: 859m / 2,818ft
OS Grid Ref: NY248048

Date: ....

Ascent start time: .... Peak time: ....

Descent start time: .... Finish time: ....

Ascent duration: .... Descent duration: ....

Total time: [   ]

Total distance covered:...

Companions:...

....

Local Pub: .... ☆ ☆ ☆ ☆ ☆

Weather conditions:..

....

Difficulty: (poor) ○ ○ ○ ○ ○ ○ ○ ○ ○ ○ (great)

Views: (poor) ○ ○ ○ ○ ○ ○ ○ ○ ○ ○ (great)

Enjoyment: (poor) ○ ○ ○ ○ ○ ○ ○ ○ ○ ○ (great)

Notes/pics:

Esk Pike

Region: Southern Fells
Height: 885m / 2,904ft
OS Grid Ref: NY236075

Date: ....

Ascent start time: .... Peak time: ....

Descent start time: .... Finish time: ....

Ascent duration: .... Descent duration: ....

Total time: [   ]

Total distance covered:..

Companions:...

....

Local Pub: .... ☆ ☆ ☆ ☆ ☆

Weather conditions:..

....

Difficulty: (poor) ○ ○ ○ ○ ○ ○ ○ ○ ○ ○ (great)

Views: (poor) ○ ○ ○ ○ ○ ○ ○ ○ ○ ○ (great)

Enjoyment: (poor) ○ ○ ○ ○ ○ ○ ○ ○ ○ ○ (great)

Notes/pics:

Bowfell

Region: Southern Fells
Height: 903m / 2,962ft
OS Grid Ref: NY244064

Date: ....

Ascent start time: .... Peak time: ....

Descent start time: .... Finish time: ....

Ascent duration: .... Descent duration: ....

Total time: [ ]

Total distance covered:...

Companions:...

....

Local Pub: .... ☆☆☆☆☆

Weather conditions:..

....

Difficulty: (poor) ○ ○ ○ ○ ○ ○ ○ ○ ○ (great)

Views: (poor) ○ ○ ○ ○ ○ ○ ○ ○ ○ (great)

Enjoyment: (poor) ○ ○ ○ ○ ○ ○ ○ ○ ○ (great)

Notes/pics:

Great End

Region: Southern Fells
Height: 910m / 2,984ft
OS Grid Ref: NY226083

Date: ....

Ascent start time: .... Peak time: ....

Descent start time: .... Finish time: ....

Ascent duration: .... Descent duration: ....

Total time: [   ]

Total distance covered:..

Companions:...

....

Local Pub: .... ☆ ☆ ☆ ☆ ☆

Weather conditions:..

....

Difficulty: (poor) ○ ○ ○ ○ ○ ○ ○ ○ ○ ○ (great)

Views: (poor) ○ ○ ○ ○ ○ ○ ○ ○ ○ ○ (great)

Enjoyment: (poor) ○ ○ ○ ○ ○ ○ ○ ○ ○ ○ (great)

Notes/pics:

Scafell

Region: Southern Fells
Height: 964m / 3,162ft
OS Grid Ref: NY206064

Date: ....

Ascent start time: .... Peak time: ....

Descent start time: .... Finish time: ....

Ascent duration: .... Descent duration: ....

Total time: [   ]

Total distance covered:..

Companions:..

....

Local Pub: .... ☆☆☆☆☆

Weather conditions:..

....

Difficulty: (poor) ○ ○ ○ ○ ○ ○ ○ ○ ○ (great)

Views: (poor) ○ ○ ○ ○ ○ ○ ○ ○ ○ (great)

Enjoyment: (poor) ○ ○ ○ ○ ○ ○ ○ ○ ○ (great)

Notes/pics:

Scafell Pike

Region: Southern Fells
Height: 978m / 3,209ft
OS Grid Ref: NY215072

Date: ....

Ascent start time: .... Peak time: ....

Descent start time: .... Finish time: ....

Ascent duration: .... Descent duration: ....

Total time: [   ]

Total distance covered:..

Companions:...

....

Local Pub: .... ☆☆☆☆☆

Weather conditions:..

....

Difficulty: (poor) ○ ○ ○ ○ ○ ○ ○ ○ ○ ○ (great)

Views: (poor) ○ ○ ○ ○ ○ ○ ○ ○ ○ ○ (great)

Enjoyment: (poor) ○ ○ ○ ○ ○ ○ ○ ○ ○ ○ (great)

Notes/pics:

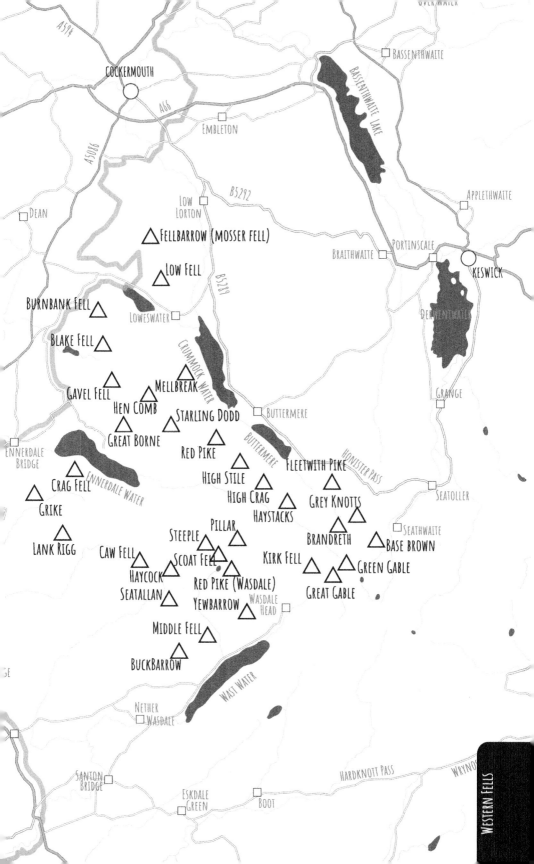

COCKERMOUTH

A594

A66

A5086

EMBLETON

BASSENTHWAITE

BASSENTHWAITE LAKE

APPLETHWAITE

B5292

DEAN

LOW LORTON

B5289

PORTINSCALE

KESWICK

BRAITHWAITE

△ FELLBARROW (MOSSER FELL)

△ LOW FELL

BURNBANK FELL △

LOWESWATER

DERWENTWATER

BLAKE FELL △

CRUMMOCK WATER

GRANGE

GAVEL FELL △

△ MELLBREAK

HEN COMB

△ STARLING DODD

HEN COMB △

△ GREAT BORNE

BUTTERMERE

RED PIKE △

ENNERDALE BRIDGE

BUTTERMERE

HONISTER PASS

CRAG FELL △

ENNERDALE WATER

HIGH STILE △

FLEETWITH PIKE △

SEATOLLER

△ GRIKE

HIGH CRAG △

GREY KNOTTS △

HAYSTACKS △

SEATHWAITE

△ LANK RIGG

PILLAR △

STEEPLE △

BRANDRETH △

BASE BROWN △

CAW FELL △

SCOAT FELL △

KIRK FELL △

GREEN GABLE △

HAYCOCK △

RED PIKE (WASDALE) △

GREAT GABLE △

SEATALLAN △

YEWBARROW △

WASDALE HEAD

MIDDLE FELL △

BUCKBARROW △

WAST WATER

NETHER WASDALE

SANTON BRIDGE

HARDKNOTT PASS

WRYNO

ESKDALE GREEN

BOOT

WESTERN FELLS

Low Fell
Region: Western Fells
Height: 423m / 1,388ft
OS Grid Ref: NY137226

Date: ....

Ascent start time: .... Peak time: ....

Descent start time: .... Finish time: ....

Ascent duration: .... Descent duration: ....

Total time: [   ]

Total distance covered:...

Companions:...

....

Local Pub: .... ☆☆☆☆☆

Weather conditions:...

....

Difficulty: (poor) ○ ○ ○ ○ ○ ○ ○ ○ ○ (great)

Views: (poor) ○ ○ ○ ○ ○ ○ ○ ○ ○ (great)

Enjoyment: (poor) ○ ○ ○ ○ ○ ○ ○ ○ ○ (great)

Notes/pics:

Fellbarrow (Mosser Fell)

Region: Western Fells
Height: 416m / 1,365ft
OS Grid Ref: NY132242

Date: ....

Ascent start time: .... Peak time: ....

Descent start time: .... Finish time: ....

Ascent duration: .... Descent duration: ....

Total time: [   ]

Total distance covered:...

Companions:...

....

Local Pub: .... ☆☆☆☆☆

Weather conditions:...

....

Difficulty: (poor) ○ ○ ○ ○ ○ ○ ○ ○ ○ ○ (great)

Views: (poor) ○ ○ ○ ○ ○ ○ ○ ○ ○ ○ (great)

Enjoyment: (poor) ○ ○ ○ ○ ○ ○ ○ ○ ○ ○ (great)

Notes/pics:

Buckbarrow

Region: Western Fells
Height: 423m / 1,388ft
OS Grid Ref: NY135061

Date: ....

Ascent start time: .... Peak time: ....

Descent start time: .... Finish time: ....

Ascent duration: .... Descent duration: ....

Total time: [ ]

Total distance covered:...

Companions:...

....

Local Pub: .... ☆ ☆ ☆ ☆ ☆

Weather conditions:...

....

Difficulty: (poor) ○ ○ ○ ○ ○ ○ ○ ○ ○ ○ (great)

Views: (poor) ○ ○ ○ ○ ○ ○ ○ ○ ○ ○ (great)

Enjoyment: (poor) ○ ○ ○ ○ ○ ○ ○ ○ ○ ○ (great)

Notes/pics:

Burnbank Fell

Region: Western Fells
Height: 475m / 1,558ft
OS Grid Ref: NY110209

Date: ....

Ascent start time: .... Peak time: ....

Descent start time: .... Finish time: ....

Ascent duration: .... Descent duration: ....

Total time: [   ]

Total distance covered:..

Companions:..

....

Local Pub: .... ☆ ☆ ☆ ☆ ☆

Weather conditions:..

....

Difficulty: (poor) ○ ○ ○ ○ ○ ○ ○ ○ ○ (great)

Views: (poor) ○ ○ ○ ○ ○ ○ ○ ○ ○ (great)

Enjoyment: (poor) ○ ○ ○ ○ ○ ○ ○ ○ ○ (great)

Notes/pics:

Grike

Region: Western Fells
Height: 488m / 1,601ft
OS Grid Ref: NY084140

Date: ....

Ascent start time: .... Peak time: ....

Descent start time: .... Finish time: ....

Ascent duration: .... Descent duration: ....

Total time: [   ]

Total distance covered:...

Companions:..

....

Local Pub: .... ☆☆☆☆☆

Weather conditions:...

....

Difficulty: (poor) ○ ○ ○ ○ ○ ○ ○ ○ ○ (great)

Views: (poor) ○ ○ ○ ○ ○ ○ ○ ○ ○ (great)

Enjoyment: (poor) ○ ○ ○ ○ ○ ○ ○ ○ ○ (great)

Notes/pics:

Hen Comb

Region: Western Fells
Height: 509m / 1,670ft
OS Grid Ref: NY132181

Date: ....

Ascent start time: .... Peak time: ....

Descent start time: .... Finish time: ....

Ascent duration: .... Descent duration: ....

Total time: [   ]

Total distance covered:..

Companions:..

....

Local Pub: .... ☆ ☆ ☆ ☆ ☆

Weather conditions:..

....

Difficulty: (poor) ○ ○ ○ ○ ○ ○ ○ ○ ○ ○ (great)

Views: (poor) ○ ○ ○ ○ ○ ○ ○ ○ ○ ○ (great)

Enjoyment: (poor) ○ ○ ○ ○ ○ ○ ○ ○ ○ ○ (great)

Notes/pics:

Mellbreak

Region: Western Fells
Height: 512m / 1,680ft
OS Grid Ref: NY148186

Date: ....

Ascent start time: .... Peak time: ....

Descent start time: .... Finish time: ....

Ascent duration: .... Descent duration: ....

Total time: [   ]

Total distance covered:..

Companions:...

....

Local Pub: .... ☆☆☆☆☆

Weather conditions:...

....

Difficulty: (poor) ○ ○ ○ ○ ○ ○ ○ ○ ○ ○ (great)

Views: (poor) ○ ○ ○ ○ ○ ○ ○ ○ ○ ○ (great)

Enjoyment: (poor) ○ ○ ○ ○ ○ ○ ○ ○ ○ ○ (great)

Notes/pics:

Crag Fell

Region: Western Fells
Height: 523m / 1,716ft
OS Grid Ref: NY097143

Date: ....

Ascent start time: .... Peak time: ....

Descent start time: .... Finish time: ....

Ascent duration: .... Descent duration: ....

Total time: [   ]

Total distance covered:...

Companions:...

....

Local Pub: .... ☆ ☆ ☆ ☆ ☆

Weather conditions:..

....

Difficulty: (poor) ○ ○ ○ ○ ○ ○ ○ ○ ○ (great)

Views: (poor) ○ ○ ○ ○ ○ ○ ○ ○ ○ (great)

Enjoyment: (poor) ○ ○ ○ ○ ○ ○ ○ ○ ○ (great)

Notes/pics:

Gavel Fell

Region: Western Fells
Height: 526m / 1,726ft
OS Grid Ref: NY116183

Date: ....

Ascent start time: .... Peak time: ....

Descent start time: .... Finish time: ....

Ascent duration: .... Descent duration: ....

Total time: [   ]

Total distance covered:..

Companions:...

....

Local Pub: .... ☆☆☆☆☆

Weather conditions:..

....

Difficulty: (poor) ○ ○ ○ ○ ○ ○ ○ ○ ○ (great)

Views: (poor) ○ ○ ○ ○ ○ ○ ○ ○ ○ (great)

Enjoyment: (poor) ○ ○ ○ ○ ○ ○ ○ ○ ○ (great)

Notes/pics:

Lank Rigg

Region: Western Fells
Height: 541m / 1,775ft
OS Grid Ref: NY091119

Date: ....

Ascent start time: .... Peak time: ....

Descent start time: .... Finish time: ....

Ascent duration: .... Descent duration: ....

Total time: [   ]

Total distance covered:..

Companions:..

....

Local Pub: .... ☆☆☆☆☆

Weather conditions:...

....

Difficulty: (poor) ○ ○ ○ ○ ○ ○ ○ ○ ○ (great)

Views: (poor) ○ ○ ○ ○ ○ ○ ○ ○ ○ (great)

Enjoyment: (poor) ○ ○ ○ ○ ○ ○ ○ ○ ○ (great)

Notes/pics:

Blake Fell

Region: Western Fells
Height: 573m / 1,880ft
OS Grid Ref: NY110196

Date: ....

Ascent start time: .... Peak time: ....

Descent start time: .... Finish time: ....

Ascent duration: .... Descent duration: ....

Total time: [   ]

Total distance covered:..

Companions:..

....

Local Pub: .... ☆ ☆ ☆ ☆ ☆

Weather conditions:..

....

Difficulty: (poor) ○ ○ ○ ○ ○ ○ ○ ○ ○ ○ (great)

Views: (poor) ○ ○ ○ ◑ ○ ○ ○ ○ ○ ○ (great)

Enjoyment: (poor) ○ ○ ○ ○ ○ ○ ○ ○ ○ ○ (great)

Notes/pics:

Haystacks

Date: ....

Ascent start time: ....   Peak time: ....

Descent start time: ....   Finish time: ....

Ascent duration: ....   Descent duration: ....

Total time: [   ]

Total distance covered: ....

Companions: ....

....

Local Pub: .... ☆ ☆ ☆ ☆ ☆

Weather conditions: ....

....

Difficulty: (poor) ○ ○ ○ ○ ○ ○ ○ ○ ○ ○ (great)

Views: (poor) ○ ○ ○ ○ ○ ○ ○ ○ ○ ○ (great)

Enjoyment: (poor) ○ ○ ○ ○ ○ ○ ○ ○ ○ ○ (great)

Notes/pics:

Middle Fell

Region: Western Fells
Height: 582m / 1,909ft
OS Grid Ref: NY150072

Date: ....

Ascent start time: .... Peak time: ....

Descent start time: .... Finish time: ....

Ascent duration: .... Descent duration: ....

Total time: [   ]

Total distance covered:...

Companions:...
....

Local Pub: .... ☆☆☆☆☆

Weather conditions:...
....

Difficulty: (poor) ○ ○ ○ ○ ○ ○ ○ ○ ○ ○ (great)

Views: (poor) ○ ○ ○ ○ ○ ○ ○ ○ ○ ○ (great)

Enjoyment: (poor) ○ ○ ○ ○ ○ ○ ○ ○ ○ ○ (great)

Notes/pics:

Great Borne

Region: Western Fells
Height: 616m / 2,021ft
OS Grid Ref: NY123163

Date: ....

Ascent start time: .... Peak time: ....

Descent start time: .... Finish time: ....

Ascent duration: .... Descent duration: ....

Total time: [ ]

Total distance covered:..

Companions:...

....

Local Pub: .... ☆☆☆☆☆

Weather conditions:..

....

Difficulty: (poor) ○ ○ ○ ○ ○ ○ ○ ○ ○ ○ (great)

Views: (poor) ○ ○ ○ ○ ○ ○ ○ ○ ○ ○ (great)

Enjoyment: (poor) ○ ○ ○ ○ ○ ○ ○ ○ ○ ○ (great)

Notes/pics:

Yewbarrow

Region: Western Fells
Height: 627m / 2,057ft
OS Grid Ref: NY173084

Date: ....

Ascent start time: .... Peak time: ....

Descent start time: .... Finish time: ....

Ascent duration: .... Descent duration: ....

Total time: [   ]

Total distance covered:..

Companions:..

....

Local Pub: .... ☆ ☆ ☆ ☆ ☆

Weather conditions:..

....

Difficulty: (poor) ○ ○ ○ ○ ○ ○ ○ ○ ○ ○ (great)

Views: (poor) ○ ○ ○ ○ ○ ○ ○ ○ ○ ○ (great)

Enjoyment: (poor) ○ ○ ○ ○ ○ ○ ○ ○ ○ ○ (great)

Notes/pics:

Starling Dodd

Region: Western Fells
Height: 633m / 2,077ft
OS Grid Ref: NY142157

Date: ....

Ascent start time: .... Peak time: ....

Descent start time: .... Finish time: ....

Ascent duration: .... Descent duration: ....

Total time: [   ]

Total distance covered:..

Companions:...

....

Local Pub: .... ☆ ☆ ☆ ☆ ☆

Weather conditions:...

....

Difficulty: (poor) ○ ○ ○ ○ ○ ○ ○ ○ ○ ○ (great)

Views: (poor) ○ ○ ○ ○ ○ ○ ○ ○ ○ ○ (great)

Enjoyment: (poor) ○ ○ ○ ○ ○ ○ ○ ○ ○ ○ (great)

Notes/pics:

Base Brown

Region: Western Fells
Height: 646m / 2,119ft
OS Grid Ref: NY225114

Date: ....

Ascent start time: .... Peak time: ....

Descent start time: .... Finish time: ....

Ascent duration: .... Descent duration: ....

Total time: [   ]

Total distance covered:...

Companions:..

....

Local Pub: .... ☆☆☆☆☆

Weather conditions:...

....

Difficulty: (poor) ○ ○ ○ ○ ○ ○ ○ ○ ○ (great)

Views: (poor) ○ ○ ○ ○ ○ ○ ○ ○ ○ (great)

Enjoyment: (poor) ○ ○ ○ ○ ○ ○ ○ ○ ○ (great)

Notes/pics:

Fleetwith Pike

Region: Western Fells
Height: 649m / 2,129ft
OS Grid Ref: NY205141

Date: ....

Ascent start time: .... Peak time: ....

Descent start time: .... Finish time: ....

Ascent duration: .... Descent duration: ....

Total time: [   ]

Total distance covered:...

Companions:...

....

Local Pub: .... ☆ ☆ ☆ ☆ ☆

Weather conditions:..

....

Difficulty: (poor) ○ ○ ○ ○ ○ ○ ○ ○ ○ ○ (great)

Views: (poor) ○ ○ ○ ○ ○ ○ ○ ○ ○ ○ (great)

Enjoyment: (poor) ○ ○ ○ ○ ○ ○ ○ ○ ○ ○ (great)

Notes/pics:

Seatallan

Region: Western Fells
Height: 692m / 2,270ft
OS Grid Ref: NY140084

Date: ....

Ascent start time: .... Peak time: ....

Descent start time: .... Finish time: ....

Ascent duration: .... Descent duration: ....

Total time: [   ]

Total distance covered:...

Companions:...

....

Local Pub: .... ☆ ☆ ☆ ☆ ☆

Weather conditions:..

....

Difficulty: (poor) ○ ○ ○ ○ ○ ○ ○ ○ ○ (great)

Views: (poor) ○ ○ ○ ○ ○ ○ ○ ○ ○ (great)

Enjoyment: (poor) ○ ○ ○ ○ ○ ○ ○ ○ ○ (great)

Notes/pics:

Grey Knotts

Region: Western Fells
Height: 697m / 2,287ft
OS Grid Ref: NY217125

Date: ....

Ascent start time: .... Peak time: ....

Descent start time: .... Finish time: ....

Ascent duration: .... Descent duration: ....

Total time: [   ]

Total distance covered:...

Companions:..

....

Local Pub: .... ☆ ☆ ☆ ☆ ☆

Weather conditions:...

....

Difficulty: (poor) ○ ○ ○ ○ ○ ○ ○ ○ ○ (great)

Views: (poor) ○ ○ ○ ○ ○ ○ ○ ○ ○ (great)

Enjoyment: (poor) ○ ○ ○ ○ ○ ○ ○ ○ ○ (great)

Notes/pics:

Caw Fell

Region: Western Fells
Height: 697m / 2,287ft
OS Grid Ref: NY132109

Date: ....

Ascent start time: .... Peak time: ....

Descent start time: .... Finish time: ....

Ascent duration: .... Descent duration: ....

Total time: [   ]

Total distance covered:..

Companions:...

....

Local Pub: .... ☆☆☆☆☆

Weather conditions:...

....

Difficulty: (poor) ○ ○ ○ ○ ○ ○ ○ ○ ○ (great)

Views: (poor) ○ ○ ○ ○ ○ ○ ○ ○ ○ (great)

Enjoyment: (poor) ○ ○ ○ ○ ○ ○ ○ ○ ○ (great)

Notes/pics:

Brandreth

Region: Western Fells
Height: 715m / 2,346ft
OS Grid Ref: NY214119

Date: ....

Ascent start time: .... Peak time: ....

Descent start time: .... Finish time: ....

Ascent duration: .... Descent duration: ....

Total time: [   ]

Total distance covered:...

Companions:...

....

Local Pub: .... ☆ ☆ ☆ ☆ ☆

Weather conditions:...

....

Difficulty: (poor) ○ ○ ○ ○ ○ ○ ○ ○ ○ (great)

Views: (poor) ○ ○ ○ ○ ○ ○ ○ ○ ○ (great)

Enjoyment: (poor) ○ ○ ○ ○ ○ ○ ○ ○ ○ (great)

Notes/pics:

High Crag

Region: Western Fells
Height: 744m / 2,441ft
OS Grid Ref: NY180139

Date: ....

Ascent start time: .... Peak time: ....

Descent start time: .... Finish time: ....

Ascent duration: .... Descent duration: ....

Total time: [   ]

Total distance covered:...

Companions:...

....

Local Pub: .... ☆☆☆☆☆

Weather conditions:...

....

Difficulty: (poor) ○ ○ ○ ○ ○ ○ ○ ○ ○ (great)

Views: (poor) ○ ○ ○ ○ ○ ○ ○ ○ ○ (great)

Enjoyment: (poor) ○ ○ ○ ○ ○ ○ ○ ○ ○ (great)

Notes/pics:

Red Pike (Buttermere)

Region: Western Fells
Height: 755m / 2,477ft
OS Grid Ref: NY160154

Date: ....

Ascent start time: .... Peak time: ....

Descent start time: .... Finish time: ....

Ascent duration: .... Descent duration: ....

Total time: [   ]

Total distance covered: ....

Companions: ....

....

Local Pub: .... ☆ ☆ ☆ ☆ ☆

Weather conditions: ....

....

Difficulty: (poor) ○ ○ ○ ○ ○ ○ ○ ○ ○ ○ (great)

Views: (poor) ○ ○ ○ ○ ○ ○ ○ ○ ○ ○ (great)

Enjoyment: (poor) ○ ○ ○ ○ ○ ○ ○ ○ ○ ○ (great)

Notes/pics:

Green Gable

Region: Western Fells
Height: 801m / 2,628ft
OS Grid Ref: NY214107

Date: ....

Ascent start time: .... Peak time: ....

Descent start time: .... Finish time: ....

Ascent duration: .... Descent duration: ....

Total time: [   ]

Total distance covered:...

Companions:...

....

Local Pub: .... ☆ ☆ ☆ ☆ ☆

Weather conditions:..

....

Difficulty: (poor) ○ ○ ○ ○ ○ ○ ○ ○ ○ (great)

Views: (poor) ○ ○ ○ ○ ○ ○ ○ ○ ○ (great)

Enjoyment: (poor) ○ ○ ○ ○ ○ ○ ○ ○ ○ (great)

Notes/pics:

Haycock

Region: Western Fells
Height: 797m / 2,615ft
OS Grid Ref: NY144107

Date: ....

Ascent start time: .... Peak time: ....

Descent start time: .... Finish time: ....

Ascent duration: .... Descent duration: ....

Total time: [   ]

Total distance covered:...

Companions:..

....

Local Pub: .... ☆☆☆☆☆

Weather conditions:..

....

Difficulty: (poor) ○○○○○○○○○ (great)

Views: (poor) ○○○○○○○○○ (great)

Enjoyment: (poor) ○○○○○○○○○ (great)

Notes/pics:

Kirk Fell

Region: Western Fells
Height: 802m / 2,631ft
OS Grid Ref: NY194104

Date: ....

Ascent start time: .... Peak time: ....

Descent start time: .... Finish time: ....

Ascent duration: .... Descent duration: ....

Total time: [   ]

Total distance covered:..

Companions:...

....

Local Pub: .... ☆ ☆ ☆ ☆ ☆

Weather conditions:...

....

Difficulty: (poor) ○ ○ ○ ○ ○ ○ ○ ○ ○ (great)

Views: (poor) ○ ○ ○ ○ ○ ○ ○ ○ ○ ○ (great)

Enjoyment: (poor) ○ ○ ○ ○ ○ ○ ○ ○ ○ (great)

Notes/pics:

High Stile

Region: Western Fells
Height: 806m / 2,644ft
OS Grid Ref: NY167147

Date: ....

Ascent start time: .... Peak time: ....

Descent start time: .... Finish time: ....

Ascent duration: .... Descent duration: ....

Total time: [   ]

Total distance covered:...

Companions:...

....

Local Pub: .... ☆ ☆ ☆ ☆ ☆

Weather conditions:..

....

Difficulty: (poor) ○ ○ ○ ○ ○ ○ ○ ○ ○ (great)

Views: (poor) ○ ○ ○ ○ ○ ○ ○ ○ ○ (great)

Enjoyment: (poor) ○ ○ ○ ○ ○ ○ ○ ○ ○ (great)

Notes/pics:

Steeple

Region: Western Fells
Height: 819m / 2,687ft
OS Grid Ref: NY157116

Date: ....

Ascent start time: .... Peak time: ....

Descent start time: .... Finish time: ....

Ascent duration: .... Descent duration: ....

Total time: [   ]

Total distance covered:...

Companions:...

....

Local Pub: .... ☆☆☆☆☆

Weather conditions:..

....

Difficulty: (poor) ○ ○ ○ ○ ○ ○ ○ ○ ○ ○ (great)

Views: (poor) ○ ○ ○ ○ ○ ○ ○ ○ ○ ○ (great)

Enjoyment: (poor) ○ ○ ○ ○ ○ ○ ○ ○ ○ ○ (great)

Notes/pics:

Red Pike (Wasdale)

Region: Western Fells
Height: 826m / 2,710ft
OS Grid Ref: NY165106

Date: ....

Ascent start time: .... Peak time: ....

Descent start time: .... Finish time: ....

Ascent duration: .... Descent duration: ....

Total time: [   ]

Total distance covered:...

Companions:...

....

Local Pub: .... ☆☆☆☆☆

Weather conditions:...

....

Difficulty: (poor) ○ ○ ○ ○ ○ ○ ○ ○ ○ ○ (great)

Views: (poor) ○ ○ ○ ○ ○ ○ ○ ○ ○ ○ (great)

Enjoyment: (poor) ○ ○ ○ ○ ○ ○ ○ ○ ○ ○ (great)

Notes/pics:

Scoat Fell

Region: Western Fells
Height: 841m / 2,759ft
OS Grid Ref: NY159113

Date: ....

Ascent start time: .... Peak time: ....

Descent start time: .... Finish time: ....

Ascent duration: .... Descent duration: ....

Total time: [   ]

Total distance covered: ....

Companions: ....

....

Local Pub: .... ☆☆☆☆☆

Weather conditions: ....

....

Difficulty: (poor) ○○○○○○○○○ (great)

Views: (poor) ○○○○○○○○○ (great)

Enjoyment: (poor) ○○○○○○○○○ (great)

Notes/pics:

Pillar

Region: Western Fells
Height: 892m / 2,927ft
OS Grid Ref: NY171121

Date: ....

Ascent start time: .... Peak time: ....

Descent start time: .... Finish time: ....

Ascent duration: .... Descent duration: ....

Total time: [   ]

Total distance covered:..

Companions:..

....

Local Pub: .... ☆ ☆ ☆ ☆ ☆

Weather conditions:..

....

Difficulty: (poor) ○ ○ ○ ○ ○ ○ ○ ○ ○ (great)

Views: (poor) ○ ○ ○ ○ ○ ○ ○ ○ ○ (great)

Enjoyment: (poor) ○ ○ ○ ○ ○ ○ ○ ○ ○ (great)

Notes/pics:

Great Gable

Region: Western Fells
Height: 899m / 2,949ft
OS Grid Ref: NY211103

Date: ....

Ascent start time: .... Peak time: ....

Descent start time: .... Finish time: ....

Ascent duration: .... Descent duration: ....

Total time: [   ]

Total distance covered:..

Companions:...

....

Local Pub: .... ☆☆☆☆☆

Weather conditions:..

....

Difficulty: (poor) ○ ○ ○ ○ ○ ○ ○ ○ ○ ○ (great)

Views: (poor) ○ ○ ○ ○ ○ ○ ○ ○ ○ ○ (great)

Enjoyment: (poor) ○ ○ ○ ○ ○ ○ ○ ○ ○ ○ (great)

Notes/pics:

Join us on Facebook!

Upload your completed pages, share challenges, routes, tips, gear, photos, maps and achievements amongst other Wainwright bagging enthusiats! We have a thriving community of people who love the lakes - so come and join in!

Search "Wainwrights214PeakChallenge"
www.facebook.com/Wainwrights214PeakChallenge
www.facebook.com/groups/wainwrights214peakchallenge

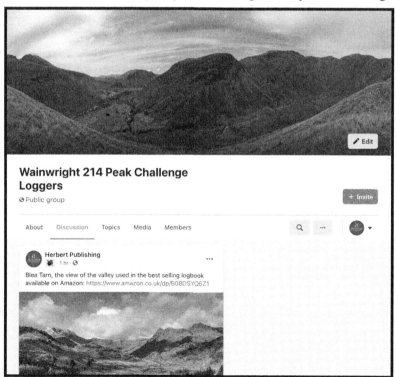

Wainwright 214 Peak Challenge Loggers
⊕ Public group

+ Invite

About   Discussion   Topics   Media   Members

🔍   ...

Herbert Publishing
🌐 1 hr · ⊕

Blea Tarn, the view of the valley used in the best selling logbook available on Amazon: https://www.amazon.co.uk/dp/B08DSYQ6Z1

Did You Know? Some Interesting Quick Facts!!!

The Lake District National Park is England's largest and covers:

2362 square kilometres or 912 square miles or 583,747 acres or or 236,234 hectares
Width (west to east): 58 km or 36 miles • Height (north to south): 64 km or 40 miles

10 Highest Mountains

1. Scafell Pike at 978 metres (3209 feet)
2. Scafell at 964 metres (3162 feet)
3. Helvellyn at 950 metres (3117 feet)
4. Skiddaw at 931 metres (3054 feet)
5. Great End at 910 metres (2984 feet)
6. Bowfell at 903 metres (2962 feet)
7. Great Gable at 899 metres (2949 feet)
8. Pillar at 892 metres (2927 feet)
9. Nethermost Pike at 891 metres (2923 feet)
10. Catstycam at 890 metres (2920 feet)

Some of the Larger Tarns...

Blea Tarn
Little Langdale Tarn
Overwater Tarn
Stickle Tarn
Tarn Hows
Watendlath Tarn
Yew Tree Tarn

15 Largest Lakes

1. Windermere - 14.8 square kilometres
2. Ullswater - 8.9 square kilometres
3. Derwentwater - 5.5 square kilometres
4. Bassenthwaite Lake - 5.3 square kilometres
5. Coniston Water - 4.0 square kilometres
6. Haweswater - 3.9 square kilometres
7. Thirlmere - 3.3 square kilometres
8. Ennerdale Water - 3 square kilometres
9. Wastwater - 2.9 square kilometres
10. Crummock Water - 2.5 square kilometres
11. Esthwaite Water - 1 square kilometre
12. Buttermere - 0.9 square kilometres
13. Grasmere - 0.6 square kilometres
14. Loweswater - 0.6 square kilometres
15. Rydal Water - 0.3 square kilometres

England's longest lake is Windermere which is 10.5 miles long

The deepest lake in England is Wastwater at 74 metres (243 feet)

The National Park includes 26 miles of coastline and estuaries

There is only one official lake - Bassenthwaite Lake. All the others are 'meres' or 'waters'

In the heavy rains of November 2009, Windermere lake rose 157cm. Over the week, that translates into an extra 35,700,000,000 litres. 22,100,000,000 litres of those were added in just 36 hours!

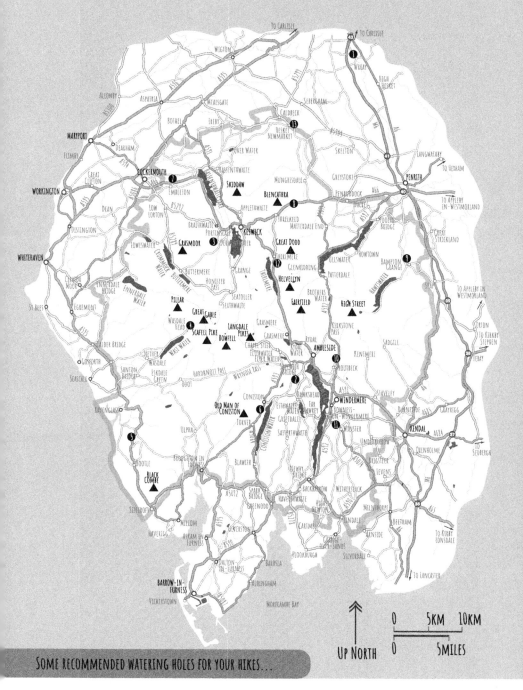

Some recommended watering holes for your hikes...

❶ The Plough Inn, Wreay
  (Vouchers available in this book)
❷ The Drunken Duck
❸ The Swinside Inn
❹ Wasdale Head Inn
❺ The Brown Cow Inn
❻ The Ship Inn Coniston
❼ De Brito Craig's Wheatsheaf Inn
❽ The White Horse
❾ Crown & Mitre Inn
❿ Queens Head
⓫ Brown Horse Inn
⓬ Kings Head Inn
⓭ Old Crown Inn

MAP LOCATION

The Plough Inn,
Wreay, nr Carlisle. CA4 0RL

www.facebook.com/theploughwreay

Telephone: 016974 57231

The kind of place which is perfectly suited for Walkers, Cyclists and most importantly Locals who can call in for a Pint and a Craic any time of the day or night.

Bar · Restaurant · Camping Pitches · Camper Van Stopovers

Tastefully modernised village pub dating back to 1786, sat in the heart of this picturesque village, 5 miles south of Carlisle.

The Plough has a well-deserved, excellent reputation for it's food which is locally sourced, wherever possible. Meals are served between 12 and 3pm, Wednesday to Sunday and between 5.30 - 9pm Tuesday to Sunday during March to November.

The Plough features in CAMRA's 2014 and 2016 Good Beer Guide and CAMRA pub of the season in autumn 2012 and more recently we won Winter Pub of the Season 2015 which we are thrilled about. It has been LocAle accredited by the Solway branch for it's local real ales. We have a real wood burning stove lit on a cool evening to add to the lovely ambience of this Country Inn.

We often have live music acts who come to entertain customers at The Plough Inn. The dates for these can be found both on the website and on The Plough Inn Facebook page.

Courtesy of The Plough, please enjoy the below vouchers to spend at the bar or on your pitch!

£5.00
GIFT VOUCHER

This voucher can be redeemed in:
The Plough Inn, Wreay, nr Carlisle. CA4 0RL

Five Pounds Only

THIS VOUCHER ENTITLES YOU TO £5 OFF ANY MEAL OR CAMPING PITCH.
VALID AGAINST ANY PURCHASE OVER THE VALUE OF £10
Excludes drinks. Management reserves all rights.

£5.00
GIFT VOUCHER

This voucher can be redeemed in:
The Plough Inn, Wreay, nr Carlisle. CA4 0RL

Five Pounds Only

THIS VOUCHER ENTITLES YOU TO £5 OFF ANY MEAL OR CAMPING PITCH.
VALID AGAINST ANY PURCHASE OVER THE VALUE OF £10
Excludes drinks. Management reserves all rights.

SOME USEFUL RESOURCES THAT ARE WORTH A LOOK

Here are some recommended Youtube and Instagram accounts that you may find useful...

  WWW.INSTAGRAM.COM/SIMPLYWAINWRIGHTWALKING

A good Instagram account to follow: Josh & Codie sharing their mountain adventures! They have created an interesting guide rating the mountains by difficulty - definitely worth a look!

SCAN TO OPEN PROFILE

   1 - Very Easy   2 - Easy   3 - Moderate   4 - Hard   5 - Very Hard   Equipment

---

▶ **YouTube** **BackpackingUK** YOUTUBE.COM/BACKPACKINGUK

Meet Andy from BackpackingUk. He offers gear reviews including hiking, backpacking and wild camping gear.

SCAN TO OPEN PROFILE

Naturehike VIK 1 tent review - Budget Ultralight One...   Hiking in the Lake District - Catbells from Keswick   BACKPACKING in the Peak District along the Monsal...   Packing my Osprey Kestrel 48 with Ultralight...   Backpacking and Wild Camping for Beginners -...   Budget Camping Gear from Unigear

 WWW.INSTAGRAM.COM/BACKPACKING_UK 🌐 **WWW.BACKPACKINGUK.CO.UK**

▶ **YouTube** **Paul Willcocks** YOUTUBE.COM/PAULWILLCOCKS

Paul makes some great informative videos from all over the UK, including a lot of popular Wainwrights & Long Distance Hikes.

SCAN TO OPEN PROFILE

Wainwright's Coast To Coast - Day 11 (Grosmont - Robi...   Wainwright's Coast To Coast - Day 10 (Chop Gate -...   Wainwright's Coast To Coast - Day 9 (Danby Wiske -...   Wainwright's Coast To Coast - Day 8 (Marrick - Danby...

 WWW.INSTAGRAM.COM/PAULWILLCOCKS46

 ▶ **YouTube** **Matt Does Mountains**

Matt makes videos on hiking, wild camping & gear - with a selection of videos dedicated to Lake District walks & Wainwright bagging.

SCAN TO OPEN PROFILE

The Western Martindale Fells #shorts   The Western Martindale Fells | Lake District Walks   The Greater Fairfield Horseshoe | Lake District...   Millican Dalton's Cave #shorts   Millican Dalton's Cave | Castle Crag | Lake District...

 YOUTUBE.COM/MATTDOESMOUNTAINS **WWW.INSTAGRAM.COM/MATTDOESMOUNTAINS**

▶ YouTube BLOT Outdoors Show

SEARCH:
BLOT OUTDOORS
SHOW

Wild Camping
Hiking Videos
Camp Cooking
Whisky Reviews

The BLOT (Bonny Lads on Tour) Outdoors Show is what I can only describe as Auf Wiedersehen Pet meets Wainwright bagging - a great channel which will put a smile on your face, featuring the three Chris's. Their whisky reviews are so funny, and the banter is canny!!! Use the QR link to access their page or search 'BLOT Outdoors Show' as their channel URL is way too long to try and type in:
(https://www.youtube.com/channel/UC6iYGA_XzZRmI2AjDgEFQ6A if you have the patience!)

SCAN TO OPEN PROFILE

Wildcamping At Silver Bay, Ullswater | Hiking And...
151 views • 2 days ago

Wild Camping At Small Water | Hiking And Campin...
383 views • 1 week ago

Hiking/Backpacking In The Beautiful Lake District,...
336 views • 1 month ago

Wildcamping at Dale Head Tarn | hiking in the Lake...
626 views • 1 month ago

▶ YouTube MCM Outdoors

Meet Chris - an enthusiast of the Great Outdoors and all the benefits it has to offer. He makes videos on wild camping and hiking in the UK, along with reviewing outdoor equipment and gear. He also offers great tips and advice to beginners.

SCAN TO OPEN PROFILE

Weather Warning 50MPH Wind & Torrential Rain -...

A Call to Action - Caledonian Canoe Adventure -...

Solo Wild Camping Adventure on the UK Fells I...

First Ever Backwoods Bungalow Camp - Beautifu...

Hammock Camping in Red Pines Wood - Classic Cam...

▶ WWW.YOUTUBE.COM/MCMOUTDOORS   INSTAGRAM.COM/MCM_OUTDOORS   FACEBOOK.COM/MCMOUTDOORS

▶ YouTube All About the Views

A video diary to look back on in years to come. Mainly wild camping and fell/mountain walking and backpacking with good mates or solo.

WILD CAMP IN THE LAKE DISTRICT

Wild Camping among the crags of Northumberland

A return to Wild Camping after lockdown

WALKING THE PENNINE WAY

A windy walk to the summit of Cross Fell

A canny day hike in the Cheviot Hills

Wild Camping in beautiful Northumberland

 WWW.YOUTUBE.COM/CHEBSOOT

Printed in Great Britain
by Amazon